The STRING Book

The STRING Book

Adam Hart-Davis

FIREFLY BOOKS

A FIREFLY BOOK

Published by Firefly Books Ltd. 2016

First printing

Publisher Cataloging-in-Publication Data (U.S.)

Names: Hart-Davis, Adam, author.
Title: The string book : an encyclopedia of knots, inventions, trivia and more / Adam Hart-Davis.
Description: Richmond Hill, Ontario, Canada : Firefly Books, 2016. | Includes index. | Originally published by Reader's Digest, New York, 2009 as String | Summary: "This guidebook covers the history of string throughout the ages, from the earliest known string estimated to be 8,000 years old found in a Stone Age settlement in England. String has impacted religions, important inventions and impressive feats, including the construction of Ancient Egyptian pyramids. The guide also includes instructions on how to tie various knots" -- Provided by publisher.
Identifiers: ISBN 978-1-77085-867-1 (paperback)
Subjects: LCSH: String – History.
Classification: LCC TS1785.H378 |DDC 677.71 – dc23

Library and Archives Canada Cataloguing in Publication

Hart-Davis, Adam, author
The string book : an encyclopedia of knots, inventions, trivia and more / Adam Hart-Davis.
Includes index.
Previously published under title: String.
ISBN 978-1-77085-867-1 (paperback)
1. String. 2. String--History. 3. Knots and splices. I. Hart-Davis, Adam. String. II. Title.
TS1785.H37 2016   677'.71   C2016-902118-1

Published in the United States by
Firefly Books (U.S.) Inc.
P.O. Box 1338, Ellicott Station
Buffalo, New York 14205

Published in Canada by
Firefly Books Ltd.
50 Staples Avenue, Unit 1
Richmond Hill, Ontario L4B 0A7

Printed in China

Conceived, edited and designed by
Fil Rouge Press Ltd.,
538 Ben Jonson House,
London EC2Y 8NH

FOR FIL ROUGE PRESS
Publisher Judith More;
Editors Hannah Boyd, Chauncey Dunford, Miren Lopategui; **Design** 'OMEDESIGN;
Illustrator Paul Boston

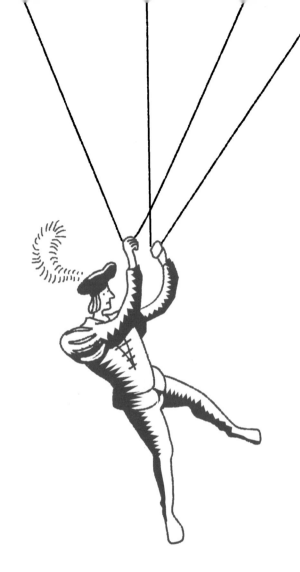

Contents

Introduction

I have always been a string and rope enthusiast. As a small boy I
strung together complex contraptions to ring bells around the other
side of the house. I used baling twine to build dens in the woods.
I used rope to hold the firewood we collected on a little cart to
take back to the house. And when I first came across the sailing
stories in the *Swallows and Amazons* books by British writer Arthur
Ransome, I wanted to tie all the knots that were mentioned.
So when I was asked to write this book I jumped at the chance,
even though I was already horribly busy. There was a desperate
hurry, so I swung into action, on a flying trapeze with no
parachute, and immersed myself in string. Wherever I went on the
train — and I had to travel often for radio and television recordings
— I carried some string with me, and I tried out my knots again
and again before writing instructions on how to tie them. I had

considerable trouble with the zeppelin bend. In the end, after much wrestling with my string, I worked it out. But the couple sitting opposite me on the train began to cast nervous glances in my direction, and after a while they had a whispered discussion and then moved away from me. Clearly they thought I was a dangerous lunatic, and the string was some sort of occupational therapy.

I learned several new knots, including the Alpine butterfly (so simple and yet so useful) and the double overhand knot, which is such a good stopper. Then I began to learn about string and rope in art, music, legends, and sports, and I was amazed at how widely the stuff is used — I am not the only enthusiast — and this has been going on for a long time.

On September 12, 1940, four teenagers out hiking near Lascaux in southwest France, accidentally discovered a cave with wall paintings that were found to be 17,000 years old. Among other things found in the cave were some fossilized fragments of two-ply rope, around ¼ inch (¾ cm) thick — probably the oldest rope in the world. More recently, in 2008, a piece of string around 8,000 years old was found in the remains of a stone-age settlement off the south coast of England, and the editor of

Get Wise to Knots If your grandma didn't teach you how to tie stoppers, reefs, bends, hitches, or loops, you will find instructions for more than 30 different kinds of knots in the Get Knotted chapter (see pages 68-105), including the granny knot (see page 75).

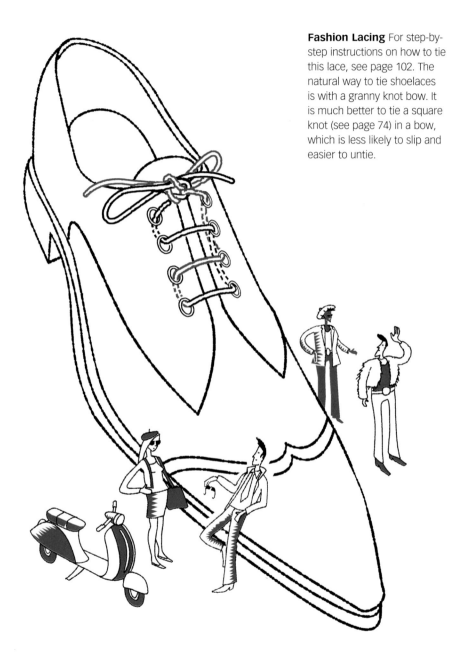

Fashion Lacing For step-by-step instructions on how to tie this lace, see page 102. The natural way to tie shoelaces is with a granny knot bow. It is much better to tie a square knot (see page 74) in a bow, which is less likely to slip and easier to untie.

British Archaeology said, "I don't think the average person realizes what an important piece of technology string has been over the ages."

Whatever your interest in string and rope, I think I can safely guarantee that you will find something in this book that you did not know before. Within these pages you will find the world's biggest ball of twine, how to do magic tricks, how to make a monopod to steady your camera, how to weigh a pig or string-roast a pigeon, seven different ways to tie your laces, and the origin of the phrase "to cut the Gordian knot."

Therefore, stringalong with me and enjoy this cornucopia of cunning and complexity. As American President Dwight Eisenhower said, "Pull the string, and it will follow wherever you wish; push it, and it will go nowhere at all." And as Sir Walter Scott might have written, "Oh, what a tangled web we bring, when trying tricks with rope and string."

I hope you will have as much fun reading this book as I have had writing it, and please be prepared — keep some string with you at all times.

— Adam Hart-Davis

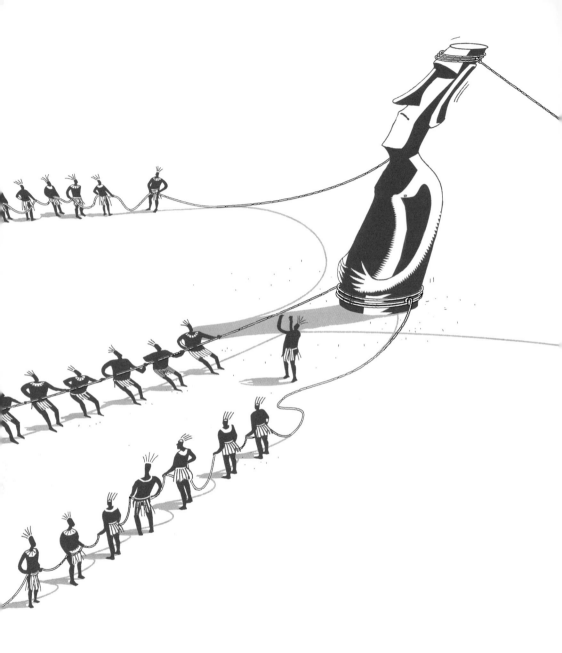

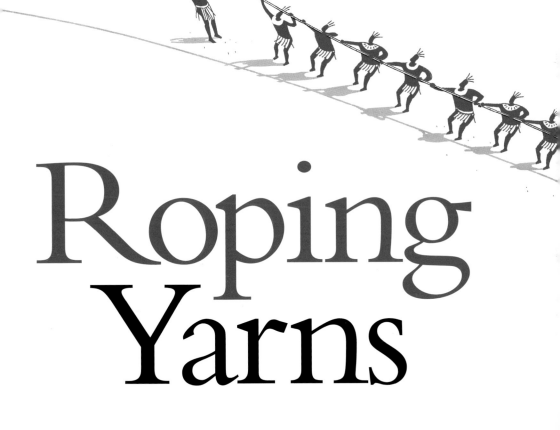

Roping
Yarns

String and rope have been used all over the world for thousands of years. They have come to the rescue of many people: sailors, farmers, hunters, surgeons, and veterinarians, not to mention boy and girl scouts, and surveyors. To discover what string and rope are made of, how they are used, and their place in history, read on.

Knowing the Ropes

The discoveries of ancient rope in France in 1940 and, more recently, 8,000-year-old string in southern England (see pages 9 and 11) prove the importance of string and rope over the centuries. But what is string actually made of? And how can a slender thread be made strong enough to haul a heavy load? The story will be unraveled on the following pages.

But first, a few stringy words that need disentangling:

Yarn Spun thread.

Cord A general word for any length of material made from twisted strands.

String Several strands of fiber that are twisted together.

Twine Strong thread or string.

Rope The thickest, strongest version of string — usually about an inch (2.5 cm) in diameter.

Lay The direction in which the strands of fiber are twisted when rope is made. However, rope also can be braided.

Find out about Fibers

Hemp rope, twine, and fishing nets were probably made before any fabric was woven. Hemp rope has been used on ships for around 6,000 years, and early ships were probably powered by hempen sails. Hemp was used in Central Asia 5,000 years ago, and by 500 B.C. hemp was being woven into fabric. And Native Americans were using ropes and cords 3,000 years ago — in fishing nets, sandals, and paddle construction.

Cotton and Silk All sorts of fibers have been used to make string and rope (see page 16), but none are known to be older than cotton and silk. As long as 14,000 years ago, cotton may have been grown in Egypt and turned into thread, twine, and cord, and it was certainly being woven into cloth 7,000 years ago. Fragments of cotton garments have been found in Mexico (5,500 years old), India (5,000 years old), and Peru (4,500 years old). Developed in China 4,600 years ago, silk remained exclusively Chinese for more than 3,000 years.

Artificial and Synthetic Fibers

One of the first artificial fibers was made by Joseph Wilson Swan, a British chemist, who narrowly beat American Thomas Edison in the race to make the first effective incandescent lightbulb. The challenge was to find a filament that would not burn out when an electrical current passed through it. Edison was convinced that carbonized bamboo fibers would provide the answer, so he sent men up the Amazon and Orinoco rivers in South America, and rivers in China and Japan, for the perfect bamboo.

Swan realized that natural fibers would always have weak points, and it would be better to use artificial fibers. He invented a way to make them from nitrocellulose — a material made by treating cotton fibers with nitric acid. His wife, Hannah, crocheted some of these fibers into doilies, which are on display at the Discovery Museum in Newcastle, England. Swan carbonized his fibers to make filaments that, in a good vacuum, could handle the current necessary in order to shine brightly. He demonstrated his first lightbulb to the Newcastle Literary and Philosophical Society in February 1879.

Edison tried to sue him, but Swan pointed out that he had been making lightbulbs long before Edison's patent. In the end, the two ventures merged to form the Edison-Swan Electric Light Company, also known as Ediswan.

The first synthetic fiber was nylon, made by Wallace Carothers at DuPont, near Wilmington, Delaware in 1935. A few years later came polyester, and then other materials, many of which have been used to make string and rope. Synthetics have advantages over natural materials. First, the fibers are much longer, which is partly why synthetic ropes are stronger than hemp ropes. Second, water and pests don't affect them, so they don't rot. Third, some, such as polypropylene, are less dense than water; so they float. This makes them useful in marine environments.

Making Rope and String

For thousands of years natural vegetable fibers — usually the stems and bark of various plants and trees — were used to make yarn, string, twine, cord, and rope. The best-known natural fibers used to manufacture ropes and string are hemp and sisal, which come from the stems of cannabis plants and the leaves of agave plants, respectively.

Harvesting Cotton The oldest of the natural fibers may be cotton, which grows in shrubs 7 or 8 feet (2 or 3 m) high. The cotton seeds are held in cases called bolls, which are surrounded by fluffy white lint. When the bolls are ripe and burst open, the lint is separated from the seeds, and the fibers of the lint are combed and spun to make yarn.

Spinning Cotton If a spinster is using a spinning wheel, she can spin only a single thread. James Hargreaves's Spinning Jenny (1764) allowed a skilled spinster to spin up to 12 threads at the same time, but if one broke, she had to stop the whole machine while she mended it.

The real breakthrough in the mechanization of the spinning process was Richard Arkwright's Water Frame (1771), which allowed an unskilled teenager to spin 96 threads at the same time, and if one broke, she could leave the machine running while she repaired it. The next step was mass production.

Making Yarn With any type of natural fiber you choose to make string, or rope, you have to twist the strands to lock them together. Cotton fibers illustrate this well, since they are usually only an inch long (2.5 cm) or less, and they have to be combined to make a long yarn. To clean and align them, the fibers are carded — scraped between two metal "hedgehogs" and then combed into a long, thin rope of "roving," which is soft and has no mechanical strength.

To turn the roving into yarn, you have to simultaneously tease and twist — tease to lengthen it, and at the same time twist it to lock all the fibers together. This is the basis of the spinning process, done originally by hand and then increasingly through mechanization.

Making Laid Rope Ropemaking follows many of the same principles as spinning cotton. There are several stages. To begin, the fibers are twisted to form yarns. Next several of these yarns are twisted together to make strands. Finally, several strands are twisted together to form rope. Each successive twist is in the opposite direction: counterclockwise, clockwise, counterclockwise again. For hundreds of years all ropes were made this way, usually in a "rope walk," which was a long, open space where the rope maker anchored one end of the rope and slowly walked backward, twisting the strands together as he moved. The walk had to be long, since the Navy demanded continuous ropes with a minimum length of 120 fathoms (720 feet or 220 m).

Using Nettles to Make Rope

If you don't have hemp, sisal, or cotton on hand, you can make your own rope from nettle stems. To do this, wear garden gloves and gather the stems after the first frost, which makes them brittle. Break the stems at the top, and mash them until you can pull out the thin inner fibers. Take hold of a bundle of nettle fibers with your hands about 9 inches (20 cm) apart and twist both ends the same way (clockwise) until the fibers kink. After a couple more twists, the kink will automatically twist itself. Put the end of the kink over a hook or another anchor, and continue to twist the loose ends clockwise, allowing them to twist counterclockwise around one another. In due course you will have a two-strand "laid" cord. To make a thicker rope, repeat the process, using your cord to begin.Next twist these together into bundles with plenty of overlap at the ends.

The Lay of the Rope Usually the final stage of making a rope was, and still is, a counterclockwise twist — to produce a Z-laid rope, as opposed to S-laid. Look at any piece of rope that is laid, rather than braided, and you can see immediately whether the lay of the strands follows the middle stroke of an S or a Z.

Rope-Making Machines Today, laid ropes are produced by machines, but they still work along the same lines of twisting and countertwisting. The first patent for a rope-making machine was granted to Americans Sellers and Bantle in 1807. Their machine was mounted in a wooden box on a wooden stake, and it was handpowered. A handle and three interior hooks automatically twisted the strands into a rope.

Braided Rope Braided ropes are not twisted (see opposite page). Some have nothing inside the braid; others have a smaller rope.

The strongest modern braided ropes are made of fancy polymers, including aramid (aromatic polyamide). Aramid is heat-resistant and immensely strong, but stiff, and therefore not good for knotting. Other types are high-modulus polyethylene (HMP), whose extremely long molecules make it tough and resistant to abrasion, and liquid crystal polymers (LCPs) such as Kevlar, which are extremely tough and resistant to chemicals.

Making Silk Among all of the natural rope materials, the one exception to spinning and twisting is silk, whose fibers are produced by the silk moth. After hatching, the larva spends 30 days gorging on white mulberry leaves. When it is ready to become a moth, the caterpillar spins itself a protective cocoon made up of a single silk strand that is several hundred yards or meters long. Fifteen days later it emerges as a moth — unless in the meantime, the cocoon is dropped into hot water, which kills the insect and loosens the silk thread. This strand is unwound and then used to make all sorts of fine things.

An exciting recent development is the possibility of commercial production of spider silk. Stronger than moth silk, it comes in nine varieties from every spider. Spiders make silk from "dope," a liquid crystal that turns into the variety the spider needs.

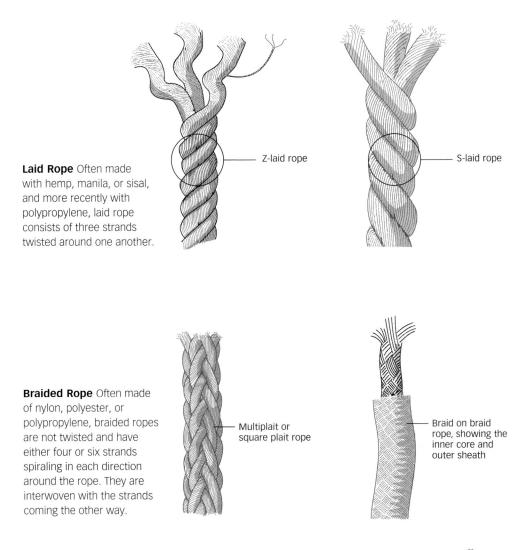

Laid Rope Often made with hemp, manila, or sisal, and more recently with polypropylene, laid rope consists of three strands twisted around one another.

Z-laid rope

S-laid rope

Braided Rope Often made of nylon, polyester, or polypropylene, braided ropes are not twisted and have either four or six strands spiraling in each direction around the rope. They are interwoven with the strands coming the other way.

Multiplait or square plait rope

Braid on braid rope, showing the inner core and outer sheath

Stringy History

String has been been used throughout the centuries in all sorts of things, from mathematics to military weapons. Here is a look at how just some of the world's most famous civilizations have used this amazing piece of technology.

The Ancient Egyptians

It is believed that rope making began in ancient Egypt. Tomb paintings more than 4,000 years old show rope makers creating a two-strand rope in the marshes — a measure of the importance that rope held in this ancient culture. In fact, life without it would have been unthinkable; in this seafaring nation, rope was essential for shipbuilding. Without rope the Egyptians would never have conquered neighboring lands, and they might have spent their days paddling endlessly up and down the Nile in canoes. On land, they would never have been able to erect their obelisks. And more importantly, perhaps, without using string as a measuring tool, they might never have planned or built their pyramids.

The Great Pyramids Surveyors in ancient Egypt used string to plan the pyramids. For one thing, string is a good measuring tool. You can easily check whether two sides of a square are the same length by stretching a string along them. And you can find the midpoint of a wall or an open space by stretching a string across and then folding it in half.

You can also make an accurate right angle with string (see box, opposite page). Early surveyors used right angles like this to plan their buildings. This is a consequence of Pythagoras's theorem, which says that in a right-angled triangle the square on the hypotenuse (the longest side) is equal to the sum of the squares on the other two sides. In this case, 5^2 (25) = 4^2 (16) + 3^2 (9).

How to Align a Pyramid The sides of the pyramids are exactly equal to one another and exactly at right angles; so the Egyptian surveyors were highly competent with their string. They probably used string to help align the pyramids exactly north-south and east-west, since they had no compasses.

To follow their example, choose a point on flat, level ground on the site where you want to build a pyramid. Mark the position with a stake or a rock. As far away as possible on the level ground, build a low wall — high enough to form the horizon and stretching in a semicircle from east through south to west. Stand at your marked point, and wait for sunrise. At the first flash of sunlight, get an assistant to place a rock on the wall where the sun first appeared.

Go away, and return before sunset. As the sun disappears, get your assistant to place a rock on the wall where you last saw the sun's edge. Trap one end of a piece of string under the sunrise rock and take the other end to the sunset rock. Pull the string taut, and cut it off at the rock. Then walk back to the sunrise rock with the cut end, folding the string in half. The fold of the string marks the center point of the line joining the sunrise and sunset rocks. Drive a stake into the ground at that point. The line between this stake and your original observation position is exactly north-south.

Using String to Make a Right Angle

Take a long piece (say 12 feet or meters long) and tie 12 simple overhand knots (see page 70) at equal intervals along it (say 1 foot or meter apart). Lay the string out on the ground in the shape of a triangle, with a knot at each corner and the sides 3, 4, and 5 feet or meters long. The end knots need to be on top of one another. As long as the sides are straight, there will be an accurate right angle between the two shorter sides.

The Groma An ancient surveying instrument, the groma was used by the Egyptians when they were planning the pyramids and laying out fields for agriculture. It also helped the Romans when they were planning their towns and building their straight roads and square forts. It is a simple instrument, but it is excellent for measuring right angles and straight lines, and it was almost a badge of office for Egyptian and Roman surveyors. Measuring right angles was very important for tasks such as constructing pyramids, creating fields, and setting up Roman camps.

A groma is a wooden or metal stake, pushed into the ground and supporting two crosspieces of equal length. From the ends of each crosspiece hangs a plumb bob — a small weight on the end of a piece of string. For it to work properly, all of the strings need to be the same length.

To find out whether you are in line with two posts when you are standing between them, stick the groma in the ground, twist it until you can look along two adjacent strings (for example, A and B), and make sure that they are lined up with one of the posts after they have stopped swinging. Then walk around to the other side of the groma, and look along the same two strings and see whether they line up with the second post. If they don't, then adjust your position accordingly.

To measure a right angle, insert your groma in the ground at the corner, twist it until two adjacent strings (A and B) line up with one side of the square, then look along B and C — it will be a right angle.

Most surveyors probably made sure that the crosspieces were fixed at right angles to one another, but rather surprisingly this does not matter. As long as the crosspieces are the same length, the angle between AB and BC (or any of the other adjacent combinations) will always be 90 degrees.

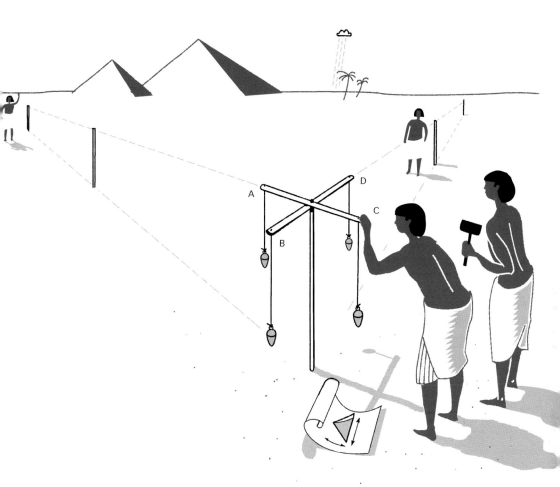

String Surveying Ancient Egyptians used a tool called a *groma* to calculate right angles and straight lines.

The Polynesians

The Polynesians were an ancient seafaring people, who traveled thousands of miles in canoes across the Pacific Ocean in search of new lands. When they colonized Easter Island in 300 CE, they left behind one of the world's most intriguing mysteries.

Walking Statues Archeologists have long puzzled over the *moai*, the giant stone statues on Easter Island. Why were they carved, and how were they moved from the quarry to where they now stand? Local legend is that the statues had supernatural powers and "walked" across the island. Adventurer Thor Heyerdahl set out to investigate, and he found an answer — it's all about ropes.

Could the statues have been dragged on sledges? Experiments had shown this to be unlikely. Czech engineer Pavel Pavel had a theory that the *moai* traveled upright, and after preliminary experiments at home, he joined Heyerdahl on Easter Island in January 1986. They tried Pavel's method on a standing *moai* 13 feet (4 m) high. They tied four long ropes to the statue: two to the head, one going out each side, and two to the midriff, one coming forward from each side.

They found that a jerk on one of the head ropes would tilt the statue sideways, so that for a fraction of a second it was standing on one "foot." If at this moment the forward team jerked the opposite rope, the statue would twist and shuffle forward — in other words, take a step. Then the team on the other side jerked, and the *moai* twisted the other way and took another step.

Coordination of the jerking was critical, but the team soon settled into a rhythm, and 16 people were enough to "walk" the 9-ton statue. Pavel reckoned they would have been able to travel 700 feet (200 m) in a day; so with a little help from the islanders and their ropes, the *moai* really could have "walked" across the island.

Pavel's Theory Teams of people jerking ropes explains how the *moai* statues might possibly have "walked" across the island.

The Greeks

String was popular in ancient Greece, especially in the field of mathematics. Like the ancient Egyptians, the Greeks used string as a measuring tool — this simple calculation aid helped them to find the value of pi. They also invented the pulley system, and used stretched strings to help understand musical notes.

Archimedes' String Sums Perhaps the greatest mathematician in the world is Archimedes, who lived in the Greek colony of Syracuse on the island of Sicily (287–212 CE).

He is most famous for jumping out of a public bath shouting, "Eureka!" after working out how to determine whether the king's new crown was solid gold. He ran all the way home naked, filled a bucket with water, and carefully lowered the crown on a piece of string, slopping some water out. Then he pulled the crown out again and measured how much water it took to refill the bucket to the brim. This gave him the volume of the crown. Therefore, he was able to calculate the density, and prove that the crown was not pure gold.

Arguably more important, Archimedes invented the pulley system as a way of multiplying force, and he showed the king

Circling with String and Pi

String is a perfect material for measuring lengths, especially of things that are not straight. So to measure pi, lay a piece of string around the outside of a wheel — for example, a bicycle wheel — to get the circumference, and mark the length of string needed. Then lay the string across the wheel to get the diameter, and see how many times the diameter fits into the circumference. That is your value of pi. The actual value is about 3.1416, but it's an irrational number — the digits after the decimal go on forever. This means that however precisely you measure it, you can never get the answer exactly right.

that he alone could drag a heavy ship by using pulleys. The more pulleys you use, the more you can multiply the force you can exert. Suppose a person can lift 100 pounds (50 kg). By using one pulley he can theoretically lift 200 pounds (100 kg); with two pulleys 300 pounds (150 kg), with three pulleys 400 pounds (200 kg), and so on. Keep in mind, there are two drawbacks to this system. First, with more pulleys there will be more friction, so you won't get the theoretical advantage. Second, with two pulleys you need to pull your rope twice as far as the weight rises, and so on. Nevertheless, pulleys do allow people to move enormous loads.

Although he was brilliant at solving practical problems, Archimedes was at heart a mathematician. One of his triumphs was to work out the value of pi — the ratio between the diameter and the circumference of a circle — more accurately than anyone had before. He said that the value of pi lies between $3\frac{10}{71}$ and $3\frac{1}{7}$, which in decimal terms is between 3.141 and 3.143.

Pythagoras's String Inspiration

The ancient Greek philosopher and mathematician Pythagoras (580-500 CE) was born on the island of Samos, but as a young man he left his native shores for Crotona in southern Italy. He is probably best-known for his eponymous theorem (see page 20). However, he was a string user, too. The story goes that he was walking past a blacksmith's shop when he heard pleasing clangs coming from inside as the men wielded their hammers on anvils. He realized that the weight of the hammer affected the note that was produced, and he went on to investigate the rudiments of musical notes using stretched strings. After experimenting with different lengths of string, he discovered that shorter strings produced a pitch that was an octave higher than longer ones. Pythagoras used his findings to mathematically devise the musical scale we use today.

The Romans

By the first century CE the Romans were already using ropes and pulleys in the Colosseum in Rome. But it was in their fighting machines that rope really came into its own. The Romans were especially enthusiastic users of catapults, which were torsion weapons — they got their power from people twisting ropes.

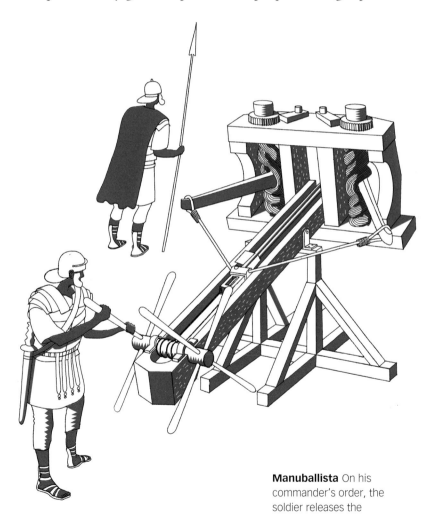

Manuballista On his commander's order, the soldier releases the capstan to fire the bolt.

Rope-Driven Weaponry
Target practice for a Roman
field artillery squad.

Giant Catapults The Romans had a variety of catapults. There was the onager, which threw stones and gained this name because it delivered a kick like a wild ass, or *Onagrus*. Then there was the fearsome manuballista or hand-cranked giant catapult. This could fire a bolt — a 2-pound (1 kg) iron-tipped arrow — for a distance of at least 1,500 yards (1,400 m) with devastating power and precision. When used against enemies armed only with spears and swords — or even bows and arrows — this field artillery was a winner. The machine was simple but deadly. The bolt carrier was pulled back with a capstan, which gave the soldier an easy 200-pound (100 kg) pull. The bolt-carriage was held on a ratchet, so that it could not go off by mistake. When the commander shouted the order "*Iacete*" or "Fire," the soldier pulled the trigger to release the missile.

The Romans went on to invent a repeating ballista, which fired several bolts in rapid succession. But it was not popular, perhaps because they did not want to waste several valuable bolts on a single target.

The ballista worked through a system of twisted ropes, or twisted animal sinews. In the wooden box on the front of the machine were two coils of rope, one twisted to the left and one to the right. Both coils could be tightened before use to provide maximum power. Winching back the bolt carriage twisted the ropes a little bit more, and all that pent-up energy was transferred to the bolt, which was then fired at speed.

The Incas

The Inca civilization flourished for hundreds of years in the Andes of South America, in what is now Colombia, Peru, and Chile, until they were flattened by a Spanish invasion in 1532.

Quipu or Khipu Most of the Inca culture was destroyed by the conquistadors, but they did leave hundreds of curious knotted strings, called *quipu,* or *khipu,* sometimes known as talking knots.

The *quipu* were made from cotton, or from llama or alpaca wool, and consisted of a thick cord with thin knotted and colored strings hanging from it — sometimes just a few strands, and sometimes hundreds.

Many researchers have studied the few remaining *quipu.* Some claim to have unraveled a numerical code, and a few reckon they have evidence of a phonetic writing system. However, what is clear is that most of the knots represent numbers.

A single digit is shown by a knot or a group of knots. So a figure eight knot (see page 71) means 1, a double overhand knot (see page 71) means 2, and a triple overhand knot means 3. Meanwhile, the position down the string represents a power of 10: 10,000s at the top, then 1,000s, 100s, 10s, and 1s at the bottom. A group of 4 simple overhand knots in the 10 position means 40.

Talking Knots The knots are believed to stand for numbers. Knotters were known as *quipucamayocs.*

The *quipucamayocs,* or knotters, were accountants, who kept records of the population, taxes, harvest yields, and calendar, and they were available to figure out arithmetical calculations.

Inca Rope Bridges The Inca people inhabited a vast length of mountainous country in what is now Peru and Chile, and they needed to maintain communications between distant settlements. The terrain was so rugged that they did not use wheeled vehicles. Instead, they employed runners to carry information, often in the form of *quipu* (see opposite page), from one place to another.

The trails frequently had to cross deep gorges where rivers had carved their way into the mountainside, and to cross these gorges the Inca people made rope bridges — the world's first suspension bridges. The greatest of these bridges, crossing the Apurimac Canyon to the north of Cuzco, the capital city, spanned an impressive 220 feet (67 m), and hung 118 feet (36 m) above the river. Although the bridge was made entirely of woven grass, it was still being used in the 1890s, approximately 500 years after its initial construction. It lasted so long because of its traditional annual maintenance and replacement by the local people.

In some places these bridges are still being made today. Once a year all of the local people gather on the side of a ravine. The men collect the locally growing *ichu* grass, and the women twist the stems into strands, cords, and cables. Two thick heavy cables are anchored to trees or huge rocks, and run over boulders on the edge of the ravine. These form the sides of the pathway. Branches are plaited and laid across them, and then matting is laid over the top. Two lighter ropes form handrails.

When the new bridge is ready, one end is anchored, and the other is carried across the old bridge to be anchored on the far side. When both sides are properly secured to the banks, the old bridge is cut away, and it falls into the ravine below.

String, Rope, and Religions

String and rope are used in many religions all over the world to both ward off evil and help count prayers.

Christian Prayer Ropes

Eastern Orthodox Christians and Eastern Catholics use prayer ropes — which evolved into the rosaries used by other Christian sects — to count the number of times they have prayed "Lord Jesus Christ have mercy on me." Prayer ropes are traditionally made of wool to represent the flesh of Christ, and dyed black to symbolize mourning for sins committed. The ends are tied to make a loop with a knotted cross — a zeppelin bend (see page 78) would be good here. Red beads are often placed around the loop every 10 or 25 knots to help track the counting. For day-to-day use, 100-knot ropes are traditional. You would normally hold the rope in your left hand, leaving the right hand free to make the sign of the cross.

Prayer ropes need to be tied during continuous prayer and only by persons of true faith and pious life. According to legend, the originator of the prayer rope was St. Anthony the Great, who tied a knot in a leather rope every time he said, "*Kyrie eleison*" (Lord have mercy). Unfortunately, the Devil would sneak up and undo the knots as fast as St. Anthony could tie them, until the saint worked out a way of tying knots in the shape of the true cross. This kept the Devil at bay — and that is the way they are tied to this day.

Kabbalah Red String

If it is tied around the left wrist (according to Kabbalah, the receiving side for body and soul), a red string is said to protect against the evil eye or negative forces. The string is prepared by winding it around the tomb of Rachel, the matriarch of Israel.

St. Anthony and the Devil
According to legend, the Devil engaged in constant battle with St. Anthony the Great by undoing every knot the saint tied in his prayer rope. St. Anthony finally defeated him by tying a knot in the shape of the true cross.

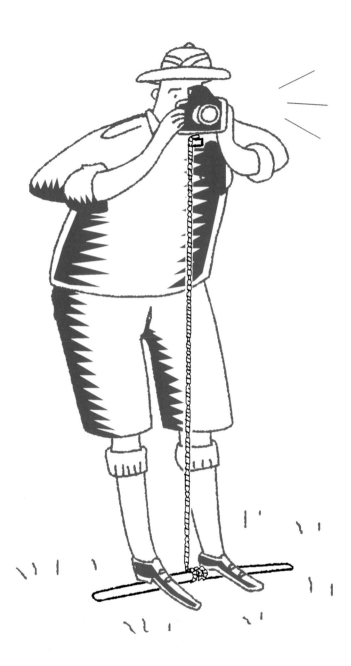

String
Along

While some sections of this book are about exotic events with ropes and ships or animals, this chapter is much more domestic. You'll discover dozens of ways to make your home life easier with a little string and some ingenuity.

Day-to-Day String

From simple household repairs to toys, crafts, cooking, and gardening, string has an amazing number of uses. So how much does every home need?

String Types and Uses

The most prepared households will have not just one ball of string in the house, but one in almost every room for specific uses: for example, the kitchen (cooking string), the garage or shed (garden twine), the home office (household string for packages), and even the bathroom (dental floss). Next you'll find a close look at all of these different types of string, and what to use when.

Household String This is the basic string you can buy in any hardware store or supermarket, and it is exactly what the name implies — it certainly holds my house together. The most common all-purpose type is made of creamy white cotton. It comes in a variety of thicknesses, although other natural fibers, such as sisal, jute, or hemp, are also often used. Household string is very versatile, and it can be used for any basic tying-up job. However, when it comes to more specific tasks, each have their own advantages and disadvantages.

Cotton is too absorbent to be used in wet weather, for example, and it is also the only one of these fibers that can be used for cooking; jute can become brittle when wet, and sisal, although strong, can feel "hairy" and rough when placed next to the skin. Hemp, the strongest and most weather-resistant of all, is usually used for garden twine.

Cooking String Cooking string is the general term for the soft, flexible string that can be used for tying up meat before cooking. It is also called trussing string, or butcher's string, and it can be made of cotton or (the preferred choice of many French chefs), linen. Cotton and linen strings are both nonedible, and they must be removed after cooking. But you can buy collagen-fiber trussing strings that are edible.

Garden Twine Usually made of hemp — the strongest of all natural fibers — garden twine comes in a range of colors, although green and natural are the most common. Of all fibers, hemp twine is the most resistant to rain, mold, and sunlight, which makes it perfect for all basic gardening tasks. Waxed varieties are available, but many people prefer to use weatherproof nylon string or plastic twists with a wire center as an alternative to the traditional natural fiber string.

Dental Floss Besides removing plaque that builds up between our teeth, dental floss can make a great emergency string substitute — especially if you are traveling. The floss is sold in neat plastic dispensers, so it doesn't get tangled. It is also very strong, and it can be used in place of almost any other kind of string. You can try it for fishing; sewing on buttons; repairing clothes, wetsuits, slippers, and tents; hanging pictures; cutting cakes and cheese; and making necklaces. I have used it, for example, as a clothesline, when I was staying in a hotel. I washed some clothes and then hung them up to dry.

Storing String Make sure you always know where your string is, so that it's easily at hand in case of an emergency. Keep general purpose string in a separate place from string that you use for cooking. Some cooks like to keep their cooking string in an airtight plastic bag to ensure total cleanliness.

Some string is available in ready-made dispensers, with the string fed through the top so that it doesn't tangle. Some dispensers even have built-in cutters so you don't have to waste valuable time looking for the scissors. Alternatively, it's simple enough to come up with your own tangle-free storage jar. Just put a ball of string in a jar, punch a hole in the lid, and thread one end of the string through it.

Home Help

In addition to tying things together, string can be amazingly useful for a surprising range of simple household tasks. Here is a string of handy household uses.

Polishing the Family Silver String is ideal for polishing silver items with awkward, difficult-to-reach holes and crevices. For example, it is ideal for cleaning fork tines. Just dip a piece of string into the silver polish, and slide the string over the area. Next buff with a dry cloth as usual.

Opening Packages Getting packages open can be a real struggle these days, wrestling with seriously strong sticky tape. The next time you pack up a box, lay a piece of string under the tape, with half an inch (1 cm) sticking out each end. Then all the recipient has to do is pull the string and the package will open.

Silencing a Slamming Door If a door keeps slamming from the wind, and it's getting on your nerves, tie a thin piece of string from one handle to the other. This will be just enough to slow the door down as it shuts. Similarly, you can use a thicker piece of rope to prop a door open that locks automatically when it shuts. This can be particularly useful if a door keeps shutting and traps a pet on the wrong side.

Making a Fuse or Taper Melt some wax in an old pan over a small hot plate or a pan of boiling water. Cut 1 foot (30 cm) of natural fiber kitchen string, and drop it into the molten wax. Stir it with a spoon, so that it soaks up some of the wax. Fish out the string, place it on a nonstick surface, and let it cool. This is your fuse or taper. Light the end, and it will burn steadily for several minutes — it is useful for lighting many candles, a campfire, or lanterns.

Hanging Things

- **Pictures.** You can use string tied around two picture hangers secured in the back of a frame to hang most art from a hook on the wall.
- **Bird Feeders.** You can hang bird feeders on strings from high tree branches to make it more difficult for greedy squirrels to steal the food.
- **Improvised Bicycle Baskets.** You can hang shopping bags on strings on your bicycle (preferably beside a rack over the back wheel — but make sure the bag cannot get in among the spokes, or you will lose most of your shopping and stop much more quickly than you expected). I have even hung a folding bicycle on a piece of string from the handlebars of another bike to get them both home.

Making Your Own Soap on a Rope Hanging a bar of soap on a rope is a good idea, because it stops the soap from falling into the bathtub or onto the shower floor, and therefore, keeps it from getting slimy and wearing away too fast.

You can buy a special liquid soap and molds to create soap-on-a-rope yourself, but you can also make one just as effectively without them. Just collect all of your old scraps of soap — or sacrifice a new bar — and use a grater to reduce the soap to shreds. Put the shreds in a small mixing bowl, and cover the shreds halfway with hot water. (If you want to make colored soap, add food coloring to the water.) Let the mixture sit for 30 minutes, then knead together until you have a plastic mass that is smooth and has the consistency of soft dough. Tie an 18-inch (50 cm) length of synthetic string or rope into a loop with an overhand bend (see page 80). Then form your soap mass into a ball (or another desired shape) with the knot in the middle and the loop sticking out to one side. Leave the soap ball to dry for at least 24 hours, and hang it up to complete the drying process.

Watering Plants For automatic plant watering while you are away, place a jug or bowl of water above the plants. Then trail a thick piece of wet string from the jug into the soil in each pot. You must use natural string, not the synthetic type — this will not get wet. To avoid mishaps, lay a plate on top of the jug or bowl to trap the string. Be sure that the string does not dip below the top of any pot, and stand the whole lot on a metal tray. Ideally, you should try this out at least one day before you leave, to iron out any problems.

Cooking with String

Every kitchen needs a drawer containing a ball of string. It can be especially useful when cooking meat, as well as for adding herbs in a bouquet garni. Always be sure to use natural fiber, or edible string (see page 37), because synthetic string will melt during cooking.

Roasting with String Many cooks swear by "string roasting" for pigeons and other small birds and chickens. Charles Dickens describes the technique in *Dombey and Son*. To begin, stuff your meat with flavorful things such as parsley and butter, cut off the neck, and sew a flap of skin tightly over the opening to keep all of the juices inside. Hang the bird by its legs on a long piece of thin string a few inches in front of the hottest part of the fire. Place a drip pan underneath, give the string a twist so that it turns, and spin it again when it stops. Baste occasionally with butter, and dust with flour.

Trussing Poultry Trussing a chicken before roasting will help keep its shape. Small birds may only need their legs to be tied, but larger birds need to be tied around the legs and wings. (You will need a piece of string that is four or five times the length of the bird.) You also may wish to lay a few slices of bacon against the bird, along the body inside the string, to provide extra fat and flavor.

Securing Boned Meat for Roasting Before roasting a joint of meat that has the bone removed and is rolled, secure it with string so that it remains compact and does not unroll. Securing it in this way will not only create an appealing appearance, but it will also ensure uniformity while cooking — untied meat has an uneven shape, which means the inside will cook at different rates. The simplest method is to tie several pieces of string around it, fastening each one with a square knot (see page 74). Make sure you don't tie so tightly that the juices are squeezed from the meat. Tying meat before cooking will make it much easier to carve. However, don't forget to remove the string before serving!

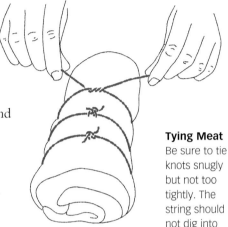

Tying Meat
Be sure to tie knots snugly but not too tightly. The string should not dig into the flesh.

Making and Using a Bouquet Garni Many recipes for soups and stews call for a "bouquet garni" — French for garnish bundle. Bouquet garnis can be very useful when you want the flavor of the herbs being used without having the herbs left in the food. You can make one by tying together (using three turns and a square knot) a sprig each of thyme and parsley, a bay leaf, and any other herbs you have available. Put the bouquet garni in the pan, tying one end of the string to the pan handle. Leave it in throughout the boiling and simmering stages, then remove it before serving.

Baking and Steaming In England traditional Christmas pudding is usually cooked in a bowl covered with foil tied on with string. Well-known British chef and food guru Delia Smith recommends tying a string handle across the top as well. Many other traditional recipes call for using string in a similar way.

Garden String

Gardeners would be at a loss without string, because it plays so many roles in the garden. For example, many modern plants are bred to have longer stems than their wild cousins, and they tend to flop over, which means that their flowers are lost and their fruit disappears in the mud, or they are eaten by slugs and snails. So gardeners use soft string — often green or brown — to tie up plants such as raspberries, tomatoes, and cucumbers to canes, trellises, or wires.

Stringing Up Your Beans To support a row of fava beans, stick a cane in the ground at each end of the row and tie two lengths of soft string from one cane to the other — one on each side of the beans. This idea also can be extended to make string grids to contain individual plants.

Supporting New Fruit Trees An "espalier" is a traditional system for growing fruit trees. They are planted by a sunny wall, and pruned and trained to stay flat against it. Usually there are strings or wires along the wall, and the young branches are tied to the wires with string, so they will stay close to the wall as they develop. The strings stretched between the posts, staples, or nails on the wall consist of either tough synthetic string that will not rot in the rain, or plastic-coated wire.

Using String for Climbing Peas, sweet peas, and some other plants like to climb up strings. Tie a string to a suitable high support — a nail, branch, or post — and to something firm close to your growing plant. The tendrils will reach out and latch onto your string, and the plant will climb up.

Planting Seeds in a Row When you plant seeds — whether they are lettuces, carrots, or peas — you can make life easier for yourself if you plant them in straight rows, because you will know what they are as they come up. Any seedling that is not in the row must be a weed, so you can remove them easily with a hoe.

How do you plant seeds in a straight row? It's easy with a piece of string, of course. Plant a cane at each end of your planned row, and tie a piece of string taut along the ground between the canes. Next, while moving the string, either make a narrow drill, or groove, with the corner of a hoe, or dig out a wider one with a spade, if you need a double row.

Creating Garden Guidelines Straight lines are good news in other places, too. Whether you are making a new path or merely trimming the edge of a lawn, the result will look much neater and be more practical if it is straight. You can put pegs in the ground and stretch a string between them, and then simply work carefully along the string.

Finding a Thorny Solution In my garden a rampant rose that had actually killed a tree and was now sprawled all over a wall, required savage pruning. Brave women with snippers had cut it away, and my job was to remove the 4-foot (1.3 m) high heap of springy rose, heavily armed with razor-sharp thorns. The bonfire was a good distance away, and I could not see how to get the heap into a wheelbarrow. So, wearing thick gloves, I slipped a 15-foot (5 m) piece of rope though the middle of the heap, tied the ends together to make a big loop using an overhand bend (see page 80), slipped the loop over my shoulder, and dragged the heap to the fire.

Cutting with String To cut the rough grass in orchards and similar places, many gardeners use a trimmer, or weed wacker, which is basically a viciously spinning nylon string. It rips its way through most vegetation up to a ¼-inch (6 mm) thick.

Builder's String

One of the most basic building tools is the plumb bob, which builders have used for thousands of years to make sure that their buildings are upright. To make a plumb bob, tie any small weight on one end of a piece of string and hold the other end. The weight is pulled down by gravity toward the center of the Earth, and the string will give you a true vertical. This is useful for all sorts of jobs, including putting posts in the ground, laying paths, and making brick walls.

Decorating a Wall To mark a vertical line on a wall before hanging wallpaper or fixing tiles, drive a small nail into the top of the wall, and use it to hang a plumb bob almost long enough to reach the floor. Coat the string with white chalk by running a piece of chalk down it — or if the wall is white, use colored chalk to make it stand out. When the plumb bob has stopped swinging, use one hand to hold the string tightly against the wall, just above the weight. Next, with the other hand, pull back the string and twang it against the wall. This will give you a perfectly vertical line on the wall.

Tiling a Floor When tiling a floor, some purists start in the middle of the room. To find the center, stretch a string along each wall, then fold it in half in order to find the center points. Take two lengths of string and stretch across the room both ways between the center points — where the strings cross is the exact center of the room. However, most of the houses I have lived in have rooms that are not rectangular and walls that are not straight. String can also be helpful in finding out if your walls are crooked. If you notice a wall that does not look straight, tie a string around a nail at one end of the wall and pull it tight to a nail at the other end of the wall. Then stand at one end of the wall and look down the length of string.

Snappy String

It is a good idea for all photographers to carry a ball of twine in their camera bag because it has a multitude of uses, including this ingenious improvised monopod. Shaky hands? Left your trusty tripod back at the base? Solve your problem with string.

You will need:
- A screw that fits your camera's tripod connector
- A good length of string
- A sturdy wooden stick

1 Using a square knot (see page 74), tie one end of the string to the screw and the other to the stick.

2 Twist the screw into the camera mount. Drop the stick on the ground and step on it. If the stick doesn't hit the ground, you haven't used enough string!

3 Roll the stick toward you with your foot, holding the camera as though ready to shoot, and winding the string around the stick until the string is tight.

4 Place your legs a comfortable distance apart, with both feet placed on the stick. Pull the camera upward to tighten the string. Take a breath, hold it, and press the shutter release. Exhale!

Stringy Toys and Games

String has been used in toys all over the world for thousands of years. Here are some traditional favorites.

Diabolo This toy evolved from the Chinese yo-yo, and it may be 900 years old. The name *diabolo* is Italian for devil, and the toy has been called the "devil on two sticks." However, the name was actually coined by French engineer Gustave Phillipart, who developed the modern diabolo in the early 20th century. It comes from the Greek *dia bolo* meaning "throw across" (as in diagonal and diameter).

The diabolo is built like a yo-yo (see page 54) — a pair of solid wheels on a short axle — which is spun on a string tied between two sticks. You, the diaboler, hold a stick in each hand like fishing rods, and the string dangles between them. If you just hold it still, the diabolo will fall off, but if you raise just one stick, the diabolo will run down the string toward the other stick. If you drop your hand fast and flick it up again, you can impart extra spin to the diabolo. The faster it spins, the greater its angular momentum, and the less tendency it will have to topple and fall off the string.

With a little practice you can soon get the diabolo going fast, and then you can start doing tricks, such as:
- Flick it into the air and catch it again.
- Swing the diabolo around the stick and catch it.
- Catch it on the underside of the string.
- Balance it on the stick.
- Walk the diabolo across the floor — can you walk it up the wall?

Pecking Chickens I first saw this toy in India, but I am sure it is common all over the world. To make it work, you hold a handle attached to a little platform — like a flat wooden spoon

— on which three chickens stand. Below the platform hangs a wooden ball, which is suspended by three strings. When you move your hand in horizontal circles, the ball swings around below the platform, and each string in turn takes the weight, pulling down the heads of the corresponding chickens. It looks as if they are pecking at the ground, one after another, in rotation.

Horse Race In this game, six horses are lined up on a tabletop racetrack, champing at the bit and pawing at the tablecloth. One, two, three, GO — and they're off, pulled on fine strings coming from a box at the other end of the table. Which one will win? Well, that depends on the sizes of the spools inside the box, which only the race manager knows. So before they start, you can bet your candy on which one you think will be the winner.

Flopsy Donkey I had one of these once. I think it was a donkey, but it might have been a dog. Anyway, it was an animal standing upright on a little platform. All of its legs are in two or three sections, and it stays upright only because they are hollow. Taut strings run through them and down to the base of the pedestal. But the pedestal is flexible, and if you press on it, the strings slacken, the joints bend, and the animal collapses into a jumbled heap. Let go of the base, and it springs back to attention once more.

Tumbling Acrobat The acrobat hangs by his hands from a pair or strings, which are twisted between two upright wooden posts and mounted in a wooden base. If you press a lever on the side of the base, the uprights are forced apart, which applies a powerful twist to the strings — just as in the Roman ballista (see page 29). This gives the acrobat a tremendous kick forward or backward, and he swings wildly over the top and then tumbles back down, sometimes somersaulting on the way.

Thaumatrope The classic form of this toy is a 4-inch (10 cm) disk of cardboard with a pair of small holes punched near the edge at each end of a diameter — in other words, on opposite edges of the disk. To make a thaumatrope, pass a piece of string about 1 foot (30 cm) long through each pair of holes, and tie the ends of each piece together to form a loop, for example, in an overhand bend (see page 80). Wind up the thaumatrope by turning the disk toward you, winding up both loops of string. If you pull outward, the disk will spin rapidly away from you and wind up a bit the other way. Pull again to bring it back. You will be able to keep it going for several spins in this way, but be very careful not to pull so hard that you tear the cardboard.

Now for the cunning part. Draw a bird on one side of the disk and a birdcage on the other. Announce to your friend (or mom, or whoever) that you can put the bird in the cage. Then spin the thaumatrope, and the bird will magically be captured.

At school we made a different version, using just one loop from a piece of string about 2 feet (60 cm) long. It passed through a pair of holes near the middle of a smaller disk — perhaps 2 inches (5 cm) across. You also can use a button instead of the cardboard disk, as long as it has two or four holes in it. The toy will now be able to spin up to awesome speeds, because the disk is not acting as an air brake. Be careful not to cut a finger on the edge.

If you make your disk from stiff brown paper with a small piece of strengthening cardboard in the middle, you can use the paper as a circular saw to cut through other paper. With this version, you can try drawing a bird and cage on the disk, just like the first type, but usually the disc spins so fast you can't see very much.

Thaumatrope Hold the strings between your fingers and twist them to wind up the toy. Then pull the strings apart to let it unwind, and watch the two pictures merge into one.

The birdcage is on the front of the disk.

The bird is on the back of the disk.

As the strings are pulled tight, the two images merge.

As they are loosened, the images are separated again.

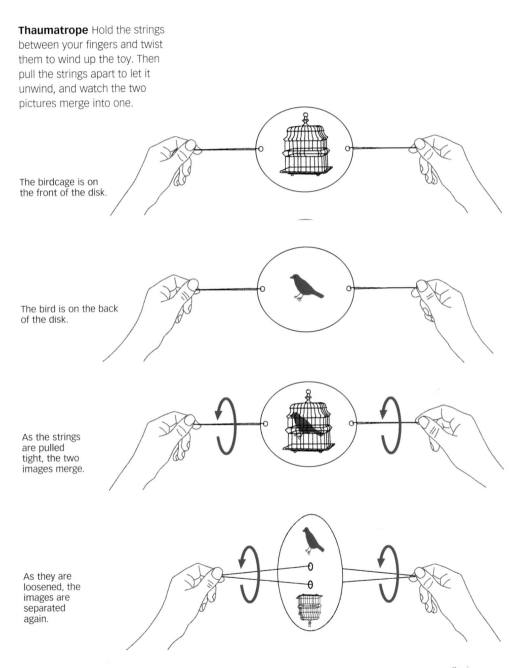

Tin-Can Telephone To create this fun invention, take two empty cans, and use a hammer and nail to punch a small hole in the middle of the bottom of each can. Each hole should be just large enough to let the string go through. Take a piece of string, preferably at least 100 feet (30 m) long, and push one end in through the hole in each can. Pull the ends out far enough to tie stopper knots in them (to try the double overhand, see page 71). Pull the string back through so that the knots are tight against the holes inside the cans. Give one can to a friend, and then stand as far apart from each other as you can to make the string taut. If you speak into one can, your friend will be able to hear the words in the other — if he or she holds the can next to an ear.

This works because words and other sounds are carried by vibrations in the air. The vibrations are picked up by the can you are speaking into, and they move along the taut string to the other can, where they turn back into vibrations of the air.

Here are some telephone experiments you can think about — or try out. Ask yourself the following questions:
- Does the phone work when the string is slack?
- Does it work around corners?
- What is the longest string you can use and still have it work?
- Does the type of string matter?
- Does the size or type of can matter? Is a bigger can better?
- Does singing into it work?

Here are some additional tips to bear in mind. With this sort of phone you can't speak and listen at the same time, so it's a good idea to use sound radio rules as follows.

Keep messages short. Say "over" when you finish what you want to say, and then stop talking and start listening. Say "out" (instead of "over") when you have completely finished a conversation.

More Activities with String

You don't have to have a stringy game to have fun with strings. There are all kinds of other activities you can do, too.

Rope Skipping or Jumping According to the European Rope Skipping Organization (ERSO), skipping began in China, where "Hundred rope jumping" (named because the rope looked like 100 separate ropes as it circled the air) was a favorite New-Year-festival sport. It has become popular in the West, both as a playground game and as a method of intense exercise or training, because a skipper can burn off 100 calories in 10 minutes. It also has become a competitive sport in which individual athletes and teams compete in a variety of events, and there are championships held around the globe. The world speed record is 128 jumps in 10 seconds by Albert Rayner in Birmingham, England, in 1982.

In 2006, a mass skipathon had 7,632 children skipping continuously for three minutes at 85 locations in the United Kingdom and Ireland. And in Sweden in 1991, Skipping Day was celebrated by 120,000 people all skipping rope at the same time.

Start with a rope that is long enough to reach from your shoulders to your feet. You may find it easier if your rope has handles with bearings to allow the rope to turn easily.

There are a variety of techniques. The basic jump is to hold one end of the rope in each hand, whirl it over your head, from back to front, and jump over it with both feet together as it reaches the ground. You can also skip backward; use alternate feet; do the "criss-cross" — crossing your arms on alternate jumps; or the "double under" — whirling the rope around twice in one jump. Then there are the "skier" — jumping from side to side; the "bell" — jumping forward and backward with both feet together, and "scissors" — moving the left foot forward, right foot back, then the other way around.

Cat's Cradle An ancient pastime, cat's cradle is a game in which a loop of string is passed between the fingers of two or more people to form increasingly complex patterns or figures in infinite varieties. String figures like this are at least as old as ancient Greece, and they appear in many cultures all over the world, from tribes in Africa to the Navajo of southwestern United States. The best way to learn cat's cradle is to do it with someone who knows some figures. But in case you don't know such a person, here is one simple starter to whet your appetite, which you can do by yourself. It's called a Siberian House.

1 Take a piece of ordinary thin string about 6 feet (2 m) long, and tie the ends together with an overhand bend (see page 80) to make a loop. Hook the thumb and pinkie (little finger) of each hand inside the loop, keeping the middle fingers outside, and take your hands apart until the string is just taut. You need to do this tautening maneuver at the end of every stage.

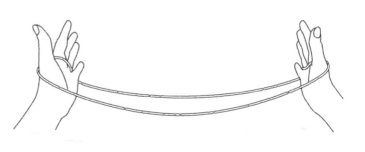

2 Reach across with each hand and hook the loop from the opposite palm with your first fingers to reach diagram A.

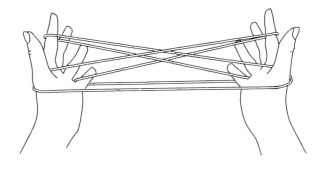

3 Turn your palms toward you. Shut all your fingers together, and push the nearest thumb string over the backs of your hands, then pull out again. Push both thumbs over the near strings but under all the others, and with the back of your thumbnails pick up the farthest loop and bring it back. Pull out again.

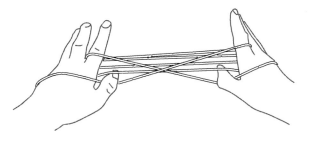

4 Keeping your fingers shut, lift the loops from the backs of your hands over to the palms, and gently hold out your hands with your palms facing you and thumbs on top. In the middle you will have a Siberian House. Next release the loops from your first fingers and pull; the house falls down.

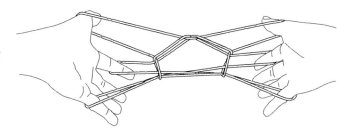

Yo-Yoing on a String The basic yo-yo consists of two small wooden disks that look like a pair of wheels mounted on a short axle, hanging on the end of about 3 feet (1 m) of string. It originated in China, where it was traditionally made of bamboo, and since then its popularity has gone up and down — yo-yoed, in other words, through the centuries. Yo-yos were around in ancient Greece and Egypt; the French emperor Napoleon owned a yo-yo, and they are still with us today.

Modern yo-yos have internal ball bearings, brakes, and clutches to enhance performance. The body may not be traditional wood, it may be plastic, aluminum, steel, titanium, or even tungsten — one of the densest of metals. The heavier the yo-yo, the more energy it stores when it spins, and therefore, the longer it spins and the more tricks you can perform.

For beginners, the string is tied to the axle. Wind the string around and around, and then release the yo-yo while holding the end of the string. As the yo-yo falls it spins, and when it reaches the end of the string, it continues to spin and winds itself up the other way. With a little practice, you can jerk the string at just the right moment to give the yo-yo extra spin and make sure that it returns to your hand.

Experienced yo-yoers (or yo-ers, or yo-ists) often prefer to have the string just looped around the axle, which allows the yo-yo to continue spinning at the bottom ("sleeping") without climbing up the string. A subtle jerk will increase the friction, make the yo-yo bite, and bring it back up again.

The moves are many and various: "Looping" is keeping the yo-yo in constant motion without sleeping; "off string" is flicking the yo-yo loose into the air and then catching it on the string again; the "forward pass" is throwing the yo-yo horizontally in front of you; while in "freehand," the string is attached to a counterweight, rather than the yo-yoer's hand.

A Yo-Yo by Any Other Name
Since its original invention in China, the yo-yo has undergone many name changes. In this case, an eighteenth-century woman is shown with an early version called the bandalore.

Kite Strings Kites were probably invented in China, at least 2,000 years ago, and they have been used to ward off evil spirits, to scare birds, to ensure good harvests, and to please the gods.

They also have been instrumental to scientific research. In 1752 Benjamin Franklin flew a kite into a thundercloud, and while taking care to insulate himself, he drew sparks from the wet kite string, showing that lightning is a form of electricity. He was lucky; this is extremely dangerous — a Russian professor was killed soon afterward while repeating the experiment.

In the early 1900s Orville and Wilbur Wright experimented with kites while designing their first aircraft. In fact, it was effectively a box kite with an engine. Even without engines, big box kites are capable of carrying people. Military observers have flown up on kites to spy on enemy positions from above — a risky sort of job. The kite string must be strong and lightweight. Huge kites are flown on steel wires, while ordinary kites usually have nylon or other synthetic strings.

Aviation pioneer Samuel Franklin Cody was the first person to cross the 20-mile (30 km) wide English Channel on a boat drawn by a kite in 1903. He later invented man-lifting kites that became known as the Cody War Kites. These were used by the British War Office as observation posts for spotting artillery during the Second Boer War and World War I.

In the 1820s George Pocock, a teacher from Bristol, England, built a carriage — he called it a charvolant — which was pulled by two kites. He claimed it frequently zoomed along at 20 miles (30 km) per hour, and that he didn't have to pay tolls on the roads, because although there were set charges for horses and horse-drawn carts, there were none for kites. He also asserted that kites would be good for adding sail power to ships and for air-sea rescue. He demonstrated this by putting his small daughter, Martha, in an armchair attached to a 30-foot (9 m) kite and flying her up a cliff.

Today, fighting kites are common in many countries in the Far East. The string, sometimes called manja, is coated with glued-on sand or glass powder. The flyer takes the kite close to an opponent's kite so that the strings cross, and then the flyer repeatedly jerks the kite up and down to try and saw through the other string.

Kite Fighting
Dueling with kites is a very common pastime in some parts of the world. The aim is to down the opponent's kite and then retrieve it.

Friendship Bracelets Traditionally, if you tie a friendship bracelet to your friend's wrist, she or he needs to keep it there until it falls off. To take it off any earlier would imply that the friendship had gone sour. Friendship bracelets are traditionally handmade. While making the bracelet you are investing work and love, and by accepting the bracelet your friend will show respect and thanks for those efforts and emotions.

One variation of the tradition says that the person receiving the bracelet is entitled to a wish, which will come true when the bracelet wears out or drops off. The idea of friendship bracelets most likely originated from ancient tribes in Central America, but it became immensely popular in the United States in the 1970s.

Friendship bracelets are usually made from embroidery thread, which is a bit thicker than cotton, but any type of thread, such as hemp, silk or cotton also can be used. Even thin string will do, at least for practice. You can make round or flat bracelets, depending on the pattern, and the patterns come with descriptive names — Bordered Chevron, Broken Ladder, Totem Pole, and so on. The simplest bracelet of all, the Double Chain Knot, needs just two threads, but some require many more. As a first guess, you will need about 3 feet (1 m) of each thread. Using threads of various colors will make your bracelet more spectacular. And if you use more colors, you will have a wider bracelet.

Although friendship bracelets are traditionally a form of macramé — a type of weaving using natural threads — many modern variants are made from brightly colored plastic string that comes under a range of weird and wonderful names, such as gim, boondoggle, lanyard or scooby-doo (see page 109). All are easily available from craft stores.

How to Make a Diagonal Bracelet

1 Cut four pieces of thread, each 3 feet (1 m) long, and tie them together, close to one end, in an overhand knot (see page 70). Anchor this end to a bedpost, table, chair back, or desk using a piece of string, tape, or a thumbtack, ideally with the threads lying on a surface, such as a table. With the left-hand thread (A) tie a half hitch (see page 82) around thread B as shown, and then repeat the process.

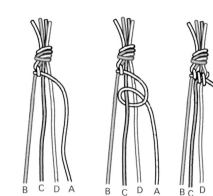

A B C D   B C D A   B C D A   B C D A

2 Still using thread A, tie two half hitches (see page 82) around thread C and then around thread D.

D AB C

3 Using thread B (now on the left) tie two half hitches (see page 82) around threads C, D, and A in turn.

A B C D

4 Repeat steps 2 and 3 with threads C and D.

BCDA

5 Start again with thread A, and keep repeating this pattern until the bracelet is long enough — about 10 inches (25.4 cm). Gather all of the threads, and tie them together in an overhand knot (see page 70).

BCDA

String Fanatics

For some people — and animals — string is not just a pastime, but an obsession. Here are some cases where stringy attractions have become completely out of hand.

Great Balls of Twine

Some people seem to live their entire lives for string. Francis A. Johnson, a farmer in Darwin, Minnesota, was a real string fanatic. For 39 years he spent 4 hours every day winding a ball of string. The ball grew and grew, until in the end he had to hire a crane to move it. When he died in 1989, the ball was 12 feet (4 m) in diameter and weighed an astonishing 17,400 pounds — that's 7,900 kilograms, or almost 8 tons. The city was so proud of his achievement that they put the ball on display in a custom-built gazebo, and they still hold a "Twine Ball Days" festival on the second Saturday in August.

However, the challenge to make the world's biggest ball of string wasn't wrapped up there. In Cawker City, Kansas, Frank Stoeber, inspired by Johnson's work, quickly wound 1,600,000 feet or 303 miles (485 km) of string into a ball 11 feet (3.4 m) across, but then he died in 1974. Not to be outdone, the local citizens got together and started a "Twine-a-thon," which is now held every August. By 2003 the ball contained 7 million feet or 1,300 miles (2,100 km) of string and weighed 17,000 pounds (7,700 kg). It is similar to Johnson's, but is a group effort.

There also is a 13-foot (4 m) high ball of plastic string from Texas — again accomplished by teams of winders. However, it is rumored that James Frank Kotera of Lake Nebagamon, Wisconsin, has wound a 9-ton ball, and is still "going string."

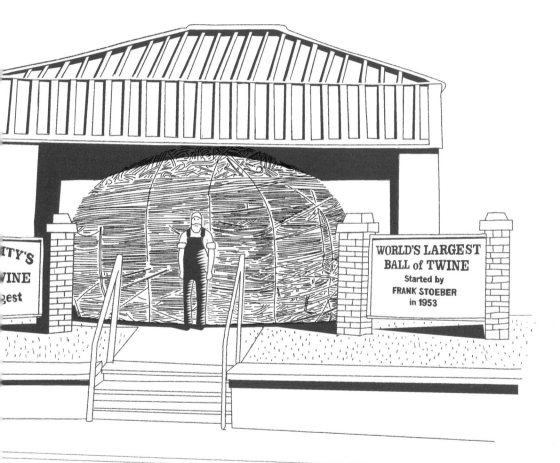

Supersize String Frank Stoeber, having a ball with the world's largest ball of twine, consisting of 303 miles (485 km) of string.

Scouting with String

The scouting movement was started in 1907 by Robert Baden-Powell, a British general. He was not only enthusiastic about woodcraft and scouting, he was convinced that learning these skills would benefit young boys and would help them to develop independence. In 1908 he published the ideas in *Scouting for Boys*, which evolved into the *Boy Scout Handbook*.

The Girl Scouts were created in 1912, and Canadian girl guides in 1910. Scouting organizations now flourish in more than 200 countries, with 28 million scouts and 10 million girl scouts/guides. Famous past and present participants include:

Boy Scouts	Girl Scouts/Guides
Buzz Aldrin	Madeleine Albright
Bill Clinton	Hillary Rodham Clinton
Harrison Ford	Mary Tyler Moore
Bill Gates	Sally Ride
John F. Kennedy	Martha Stewart
Ronald Reagan	Queen Elizabeth II
Mark Spitz	Celine Dion
Pierre Trudeau	Karen Kain

Scouting and guiding are all about practical outdoor activities, many of which involve string or rope and knots. Camping, sailing, rappelling, and rock climbing all need ropes and knots, and there are special high rope courses, which are suitable for the fearless. In fact, knots are so important to scouts that their awards are patches embroidered with square knots.

The scouts' motto is "Be prepared." One obvious way to be prepared is to carry a piece of string with you at all times — and you don't have to be a scout to do that.

The Friendship Knot This ornamental bend has been traditionally used for tying together the ends of scouts' neckerchiefs, but you might like to use it to tie a friendship bracelet (see page 58) onto your friend's wrist.

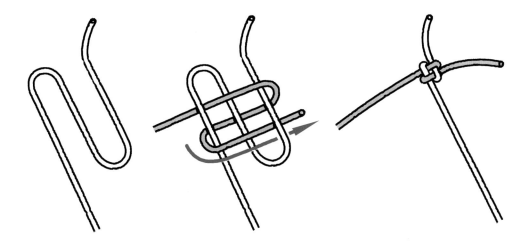

1 Lay one end of the neckerchief or bracelet on a table in a zig-zag S-shape to make two loops.

2 Take the other end up through the first loop from below, over two, all the way around underneath, over two, and down through the second loop.

3 Gently pull all four ends until the knot sets down into a square, symmetrical shape.

Cats and String

Cats love string. If you walk across the floor trailing a piece of string, your cat will wake up, or even stop washing, and pounce. If you walk briskly into the next room, the cat will bound after you as though lunch was being served. This seems to be an instinctive hunting reaction: Kittens will chase the twitching ends of balls of wool; their parents will go for anything from a scarf to a rope.

Perhaps the most spectacular display comes if you drag the string over the cat's back, even when the end has been captured. At this point my cats roll over and wrestle furiously with all four paws, chewing at the end. One cat, Inky, was particularly fond of thin, stranded polypropylene string. She would grip it in her teeth 8 inches (20 cm) from the end and systematically shred it. Even better, if the end was knotted she would enthusiastically rip it apart right down to the knot, and then dump the string in a state of happy fulfillment.

However, many cats suffer badly after swallowing string. One Siamese kitten, taken to the vet because it was vomiting, had a 4-inch (10-cm) piece of string wrapped around its tongue and a substantial ball knotted and lodged in its gut. The cat recovered after surgery, but it was a close call.

Important lesson:
Don't leave your cat alone with string. It could be fatal.

Cat-Astrophe Cats often tangle with string — with disastrous consequences.

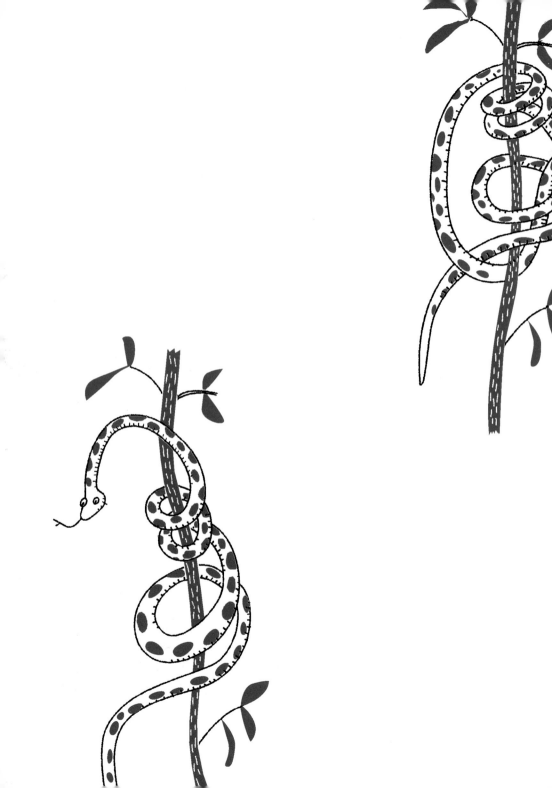

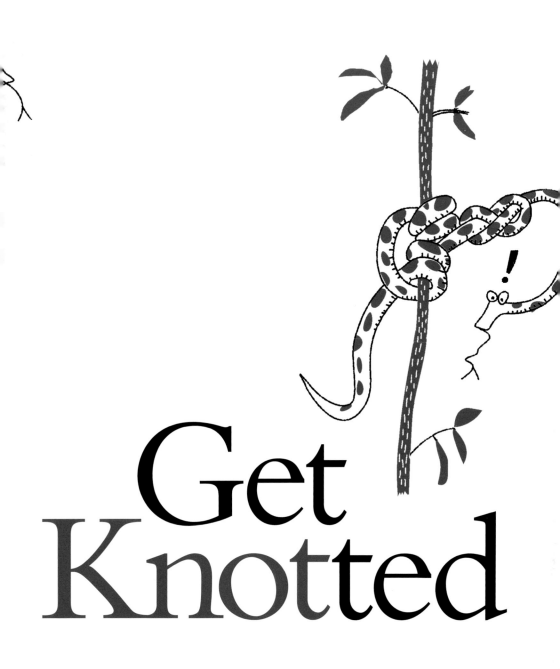

Get
Knotted

String is a clever material. You can make shapes and patterns and play games with it, but if you want to do anything useful, you have to use knots. Knots are the cunning, twisty things that fix the string to itself or to anything else, from an earring to an elephant.

Knots

There are separate knots for various purposes, and in this chapter you will find out the specific uses for each knot and how to tie them. The simplest ones are generally found at the beginning of each section, but you will be able to tie all of them if you follow the step-by-step instructions.

String Types and Uses

Each group of knots has its own section. You will soon discover that stopper knots are the simple knots you tie at the end of a piece of string. Reefs are the knots you use to secure packages. Bends are for tying two strings or ropes together; while hitches are for tying string or rope to solid objects. And last of all, loops are for looping your string or rope around pegs, posts and people.

Knots Made Simple Take a piece of string and tie a knot, and it seems obvious. Read the instructions for tying a knot in a big knot handbook, however, and it may seem impossibly complicated. Try this, for example:

Make a crossing turn by taking the bight over the standing parts…

Since I never was a Boy Scout, a serious sailor, or a climber, I learned all my knots from storybooks and from friends, and the ones that I remember and tie are the knots that were the most useful.

In this book the knots are all easy to tie, useful, and — most important of all — fun. I have kept the instructions simple, and I have worked through every knot myself, so I am confident that you will be able to tie them.

However, in case you want to look up other knots in a knot book, here are some basic technical terms you may want to know.

Standing End or Part. The long end of a piece of string — the end you are not usually going to use to tie a knot. In the pages that follow it is called the long end.

Working End. This is the end of the string that you are working with, but unfortunately it's not always obvious. In this book the working end is called the loose end.

Short End. Most knots are tied near one end of a piece of string, and the short end is usually the one that you are using (the loose end in these pages, see above).

Bight. This is a simple loop in the string, where the ends don't cross.

Crossing Loop. And this is a loop where the ends do cross.

Drawloop. Simple stopper knots sometimes jam, which can be very annoying. The cunning way to avoid this is to use a drawloop. Tie it by making an overhand knot (see page 70) without pulling the loose end right through the loop; untie it easily by pulling the loose end. Use the same trick with a figure eight and other stoppers. The highwayman's hitch (see page 89) is an example of an advanced drawloop.

Jam. This term often refers to the sweet stuff you put on bread, or too much traffic on the road. In this book it is what you don't want knots to do — jam so tight that you can't undo them. If you want to see a jam, wet a piece of white kitchen string, tie an overhand knot (see page 70), and pull it really tight. Then try to undo it — but don't get too uptight.

Bind. This is a bit like jamming, but it is good news instead of bad. You want a knot to be secure; it needs to hold without slipping even under tension. A good knot will actually tighten on itself and grip more securely when pulled, but without jamming. That is called binding.

That's more than you need to know about the theory. All you need now is some practice — and a piece of string. Happy knotting!

Stoppers

Tie a stopper knot at the end of a piece of rope or string to stop it from slipping back through a hole or eyelet. If you have a string you don't want to unravel, this kind of knot will stop the string from fraying at the end.

Overhand Knot

- The simplest knot of all, the overhand is the basis of many knots in this book.

- It is usually enough of a stopper to prevent the end of a length of thread from slipping through the eye of a needle.

- You can also use an overhand knot to contain loose change inside a handkerchief.

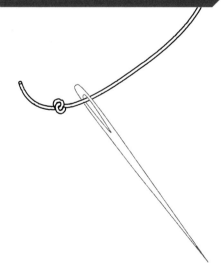

1 Make a small loop near the loose end of your string, and tuck the loose end through the loop.

2 Pull both ends to tighten.

Double Overhand Knot

Slightly chunkier and less likely to jam than a simple overhand type, this version involves making one extra turn with the loose end through the loop.

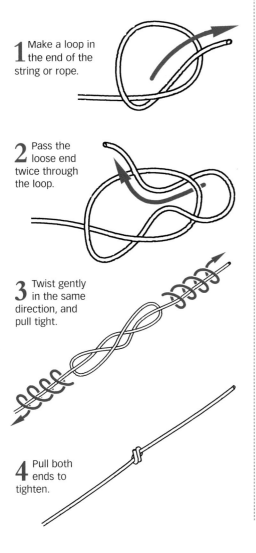

1 Make a loop in the end of the string or rope.

2 Pass the loose end twice through the loop.

3 Twist gently in the same direction, and pull tight.

4 Pull both ends to tighten.

Figure Eight Knot

- One step beyond an overhand knot.
- It is a popular knot with sailors and climbers because it's quick and easy to tie and fairly easy to untie.
- As a loose knot, it is a symbol of undying love.

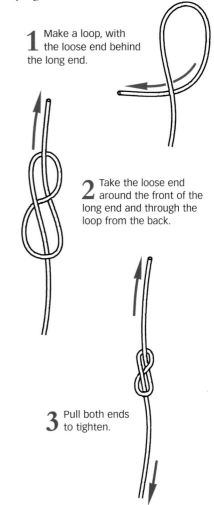

1 Make a loop, with the loose end behind the long end.

2 Take the loose end around the front of the long end and through the loop from the back.

3 Pull both ends to tighten.

Stevedore Knot

- A bulkier knot than the overhand or the figure eight, the stevedore does not jam.
- The opposite of the double overhand knot, it has one extra turn by the loose end outside the loop.
- It gained the name because it was often used by stevedores or dockworkers.

1 Make a loop in the rope. Pass the loose end once around the long end.

2 Pass the loose end around the long end a second time.

3 Pass the loose end back through the loop.

4 Pull both ends to tighten.

Ashley's Stopper Knot

- If you want a really bulky knot, for example, to tie tarpaulins down, Clifford Ashley's is the stopper for you.

- Ashley designed his stopper knot in 1910 after seeing a similar one in use on an oyster boat. For that reason, it is sometimes called an oysterman's knot.

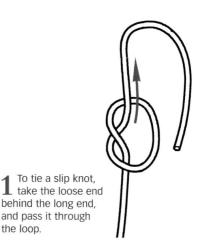

1 To tie a slip knot, take the loose end behind the long end, and pass it through the loop.

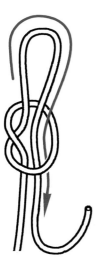

2 Pass the loose end from front to back through the center loop.

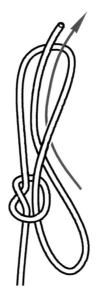

3 Take the loose end back through the new loop.

4 Pull both ends to tighten the knot.

Reefs

Reef knots are used to tie together the two ends of a single piece of string or rope. They are not good for tying two separate pieces of string together — for that you need a bend.

Square Knot

- Originally used to reef sails on ships, this is the standard package knot you use to tie two ends together against a flat surface.

- It is easy to tie and untie.

- Although it is excellent for shoelaces, it is not recommended for tying two ropes together, or for tying rope to any solid object.

- If you pull it from one long end only, the knot can slide loose.

1 Bring the two ends of string together, and bring left over right.

2 Turn the loose ends around, and twist the right over the left.

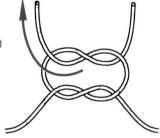

In the Loop

This is one of the few knots that you can use to tie string or rope ends together under tension. If you are tying up a package, for instance, complete step 1 above, pulling the ends apart, then lock the twist temporarily by pressing it with a finger while you complete step 2. You will need both hands to pull the ends. If there is someone else around, ask him to press and carefully complete the knot underneath his finger.

3 Pull both loose ends to tighten.

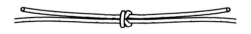

4 To make the knot more secure, tape both loose ends to their long ends.

Granny Knot or Grief Knot

- The poor relation of the reef knot family, which is why it is called the grief or thief knot.

- This common knot highlights why you need to learn other knots. Its draw-backs are that it often slips, can easily become undone, and sometimes jams.

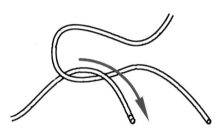

1 With two pieces of string, bring the two loose ends together.

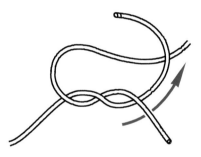

2 To tie a granny knot, twist left over right then left over right again.

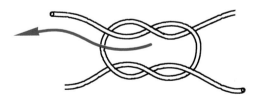

3 Then twist left over right again and pull to tighten both loose ends.

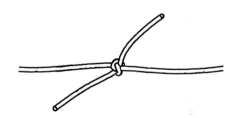

4 In a square knot the loose ends lie beside the long ends of the rope; in a granny the loose ends stick out at ugly angles.

Bends

You use bends for tying two ropes or strings together. The verb "to bend" used to mean to restrain with a bond or to bend a bow with its bowstring. Today, in the case of knots, it means "to join two ropes."

Carrick Bend

- Saxon chief Hereward the Wake, who led a revolutionary attack on William the Conqueror's Norman army in 1070 and 1071, used the Carrick bend as a heraldic symbol.

- When loosely tied, this bend looks pretty, so it is often used in decorative ropework.

- It is a good way to join two ropes, even if they are different thicknesses, because when you pull it tight, the knot binds securely but does not jam, and therefore, you can untie it easily.

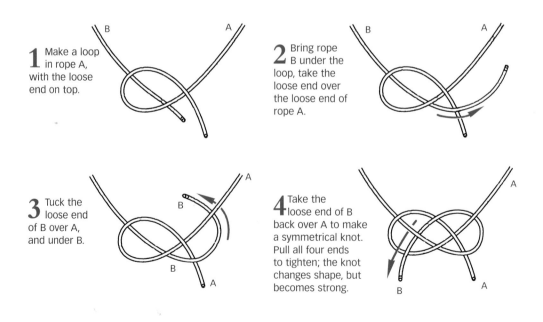

1 Make a loop in rope A, with the loose end on top.

2 Bring rope B under the loop, take the loose end over the loose end of rope A.

3 Tuck the loose end of B over A, and under B.

4 Take the loose end of B back over A to make a symmetrical knot. Pull all four ends to tighten; the knot changes shape, but becomes strong.

Fisherman's Knot

- A simple joining knot, the fisherman's knot is safe for rope and string — even fishing line — as long as the two pieces are the same thickness.

- This knot tends to jam with fine string, and you may be unable to untie it.

1 Lay the two strings side by side with the loose ends pointing in opposite directions. With the loose end of string A, tie an overhand knot (see page 70) around string B, so that the loose end remains parallel to B. With the loose end of B, tie an overhand knot around A, with the loose end parallel to A.

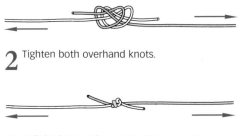

2 Tighten both overhand knots.

3 Pull the long ends to bring them snugly together.

Double Fisherman's Knot

A more secure form of the fisherman's knot, this version makes use of double overhand knots (see page 71) instead of single ones.

1 To make this knot more secure, tape the loose ends to the long ends or tie double overhand knots at each end.

2 Take the loose ends back through the second loops.

3 Pull both ends to tighten.

Zeppelin Bend or Rosendahl Bend

- Charles Rosendahl was an airship captain, and he was convinced that this knot was the strongest and most secure of all bends. Apparently, he insisted that no other knot would do for tethering his airship, although why he was not using a hitch remains a mystery.

- The original airships were built by Count Ferdinand von Zeppelin in the 1890s. German airships were named zeppelins after him, so the name stuck to the knot as well.

1 Make identical loops, loose end on top, in the end of each rope.

2 Give the right loop a twist, to take the loose end under. The loops should look like "p" and "q."

3 Lay the left loop on top, so that the loose ends are on top and bottom.

4 Take the upper loose end around and through the double loop from below and the lower loose end around and through the double loop from above.

5 Pull tight. The loose ends will stick out at right angles from the long ends.

Flemish Bend

- A neat and secure way of joining two ropes, this bend is often used by climbers.

- With modern synthetic ropes, the bend does not jam and is easy to untie; but old sea dogs dislike it, because with natural rope it tends to jam.

1 Form a loose figure eight knot (see page 71) in the first rope.

2 With the loose end of the second rope, follow the figure eight backward alongside the first rope.

3 Try to keep to the outside of the bottom loop and the inside of the top one.

4 Take the second rope back down under both itself and the first rope.

5 Cross the second rope back over itself and the bottom loop of the first rope. Feed it under the bottom strands of both bottom loops.

6 Pull all ends to tighten.

Overhand Bend

A simple, easy-to-tie bend, this knot is popular with climbers.

1 Lay the two loose ends together, and tie an overhand knot (see page 70) with both.

2 Pull tight, first with the long ends together against the short ends, and then long end against long end.

Sheet Bend and Double Sheet Bend

- Sheet bends are useful for tying together two strings or two ropes of different thicknesses.

- The double sheet bend is a much more secure choice, especially if one string is much thicker than the other.

1 Make a loop in the loose end of the thicker rope.

2 Take the thinner loose end up through the loop from behind, around the back of both ends of the thick string, and across the front, tucking it under itself. Note that both the loose ends will be on the same side of the knot.

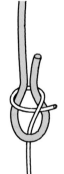

3 For a double sheet bend, take the thin loose end twice around, tucking it under each time.

4 Pull both ends to tighten.

Diamond Knot

Scouts use this complex, but attractive, knot to tie together the ends of a loop of string to carry a knife or whistle.

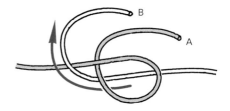

1 Make a loop in rope A with the loose end underneath, and bring the loose end of B under the loop and over the long end of A.

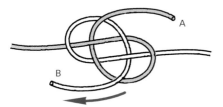

2 Carry around the loose end of B, under A, over A, under B, and over A again.

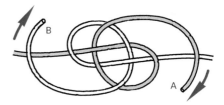

3 Take each loose end over the long end of the other string and then up through the hole in the middle. Gently pull tight, and work out loose sections from the middle, until the loose ends lie together and on the opposite side of the knot to the long ends.

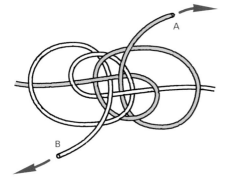

4 Carry around the loose end of B, under A, over A, under B, and over A again.

5 Pull both ends to tighten.

Hitches

Hitches are used to tie strings or ropes to solid objects — rings, keys, posts, and trees. Often you need to tie a hitch knot quickly, and sometimes you need to untie it quickly, so it is usually easy to tie and untie.

Half Hitch or Single Hitch

This is the simplest way to tie a rope to a rail, post, or ring. A half hitch is quick and easy to tie, but not secure — pull, and it may come undone.

1 Pass the loose end around the rail, from the back to the front.

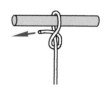

2 Take the loose end around behind the long end and through the loop you have made. Pull the loose end tight.

Clove Hitch

- This is a very common binding knot you can use to secure light boats or suspend light items.

- The ease with which you can tie this knot makes it popular, but it is not very secure, and it can come adrift if pulled and jerked apart.

- The knot is only secure if an equal load is put on both sides of the knot.

- When ashore, this is commonly known as a builder's knot.

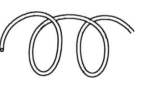

1 Form two similarly sized loops in a length of rope, with the loose end passing twice over the long end.

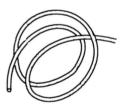

2 Bring the two loops together, right on top of left, overlapping them to form a circle.

3 Insert a pole into the circle, or place the circle over a post or rail. Make sure that the loose end protrudes from the opposite side of the knot to the long end. Pull tight on the long end to secure the knot.

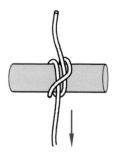

Cow Hitch and Pedigree Cow Hitch

- Even if you don't have a cow, this is a useful knot for tying anything loosely to a rail, post, or ring when you want the rope to meet it at a right angle.

- The pedigree variation is more secure than the cow hitch and retains its strength regardless of the direction or angle of pull; it doesn't slip either.

- A pedigree hitch is a convenient way to start a lashing (see page 168) or to suspend garden and garage implements from a ceiling.

1 Pass the loose end of the rope around the rail, working from front to back — then to the front again — forming a loop.

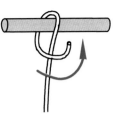

2 Bring the loose end in front of the main rope, under the rail, and back over the rail, from the back to the front.

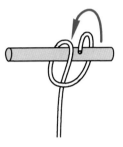

3 Pass the loose end over the pole and cross inside the long end to form a second loop and complete the cow hitch.

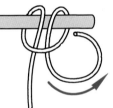

4 For the pedigree, feed the loose end along the front of the rail, through the double loop. Pull both ends tight to secure the knot.

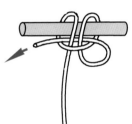

In the Loop

The cow hitch has the advantage of being tied with a closed loop, such as an elastic band. Feed a loop of the band through a key ring, for example, pull the loop through the rest of the band, and you have a secure knot. However, if the string is not a closed loop, the hitch may slip, and you can use the pedigree cow hitch (see step 4).

Taut-Line Hitch

- When you want to tie a rope to a tent peg, or a post, and you may need to make the rope tighter or looser later, this is the hitch to use. The knot slides easily when it is loose, but holds well when it is under tension.

- The taut-line hitch is a great choice if you want to secure tarpaulins.

- This knot was used by astronauts on a space mission to repair the Hubble Space Telescope.

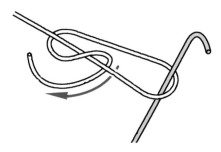

1 Make a loop of rope around your tent peg or post, keeping a long loose end.

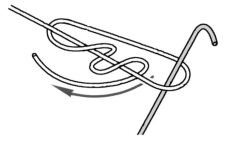

2 Pass the loose end twice through the loop.

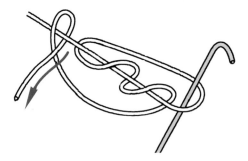

3 Take the loose end over the long end beyond the loop and back down through the new loop you have just formed.

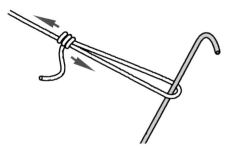

4 Pull the loose end to tighten the knot, which will then slide up and down the long end, but not slip when you pull the long end.

Anchor Bend

- A useful, secure way to fasten a rope to an anchor, rail, post, or ring, or to tie a string to a ring, pencil, finger, or door handle.

- True to its name, the anchor bend will not slip, and it is fairly easy to untie.

- The anchor bend is closely related to the round turn and two half hitches (see page 86), but it is more secure and slightly trickier to tie.

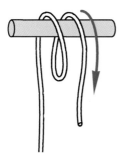

1 Pass your string or rope loosely around the rail or through the ring, starting at the back, then around again.

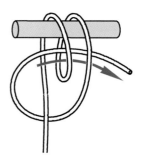

2 Pass the loose end behind the long end and through the double loop you have formed.

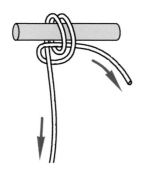

3 Pull both ends to tighten.

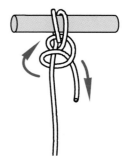

4 Pass the loose end behind the long end again and through the new loop you have just made. Pull tight once more.

Round Turn and Two Half Hitches

- This knot sequence is a safe way to fasten a rope to a post or rail, or to tie a string to a chair leg, finger, or door handle.

- The combination will not slip, and it is fairly easy to untie.

- A round turn and two half hitches is one of the best ways of tethering a boat, dog, or horse securely while it is pulling on the rope.

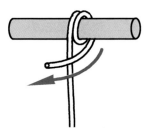

1 Pass your string or rope around the rail or through the ring, starting at the back, and then around again. If the rope is being pulled, clamp it to the post with your free hand.

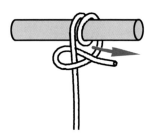

2 Pass the loose end behind the long end and then through the single loop you have just formed.

3 Pull both ends to tighten. This is a half hitch.

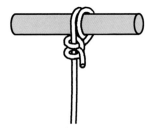

4 Pass the loose end behind the long end again and through the new loop you have just made. Pull both ends to tighten.

Timber Hitch and Killick Hitch

- The timber hitch is a quick — and simple — knot that loggers use to haul logs and tree trunks along the ground and up onto trucks.

- The timber hitch plus an extra half hitch makes a killick hitch.

- A killick was a light anchor, or just a heavy stone used as an anchor, and the killick hitch was used by boatmen as a quick mooring knot.

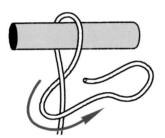

1 Pass the rope around the log to make a loop.

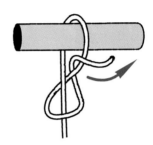

2 Pass the loose end through the loop three or four times. Making this sort of sliding noose is called glogging.

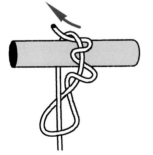

3 Pull the long end to tighten the noose.

4 To make a killick hitch, form another half hitch around the log or pole, near the end you want to pull. Pull to tighten.

Blake's Hitch

- This knot first appeared in 1981 in an Austrian caving magazine. However, it is named after Jason Blake, who wrote about it in an arborist's magazine.

- Cavers and climbers use Blake's hitch to maneuver up and down vertical ropes, because it can grip fast without binding.

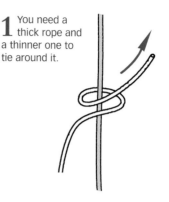

1 You need a thick rope and a thinner one to tie around it.

2 Coil the loose end of your thinner rope loosely four times around the thick rope.

3 Take the loose end down below the long end of your thin rope, behind the thick rope, and up through two of the four coils.

4 Pull both ends tight, and for safety's sake tie a figure eight (see page 71) or an overhand knot (see page 70) in the loose end to stop it from slipping back. You will now be able to slide the knot up and down easily, but when you pull down, the knot will grip the thick rope tightly without slipping.

Highwayman's Hitch

- Highwaymen used this knot to tether their horses when they thought they might have to make a quick getaway. It is useful, too, for bank robbers in the movies planning their escape on horseback or by speedboat.

- Beware, however, because the knot is not secure. It may slip and come undone all by itself.

1 Make a long loop of rope behind a fixed bar, post, or ring.

2 Make a second loop from the long end and push it up in front of the bar and then through the first loop.

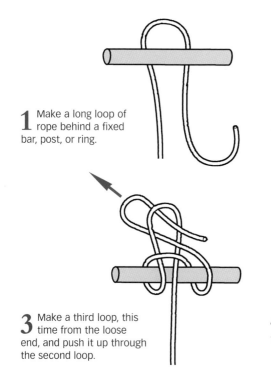

3 Make a third loop, this time from the loose end, and push it up through the second loop.

4 Pull on the long end to tighten loop 2 and trap loop 3.

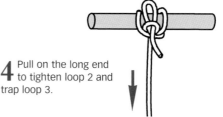

Loops

You can use loops for various things, and many can act as bends or hitches. For example, you can drop a bowline over a post to act as a hitch, while two ropes can be joined together by making a bowline in the end of each so that they interlock.

Simple Noose

- The simplest of running (sliding) loops, you can use a noose as the basis for more complex knots.

- You can start simple lashings (see page 168) with this knot, and also use it for tying packages.

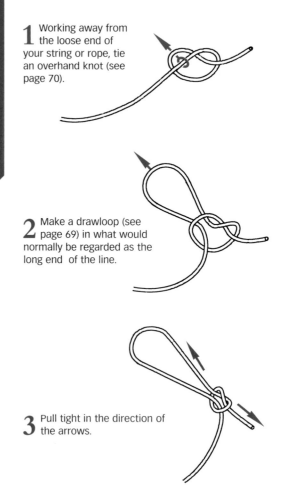

1 Working away from the loose end of your string or rope, tie an overhand knot (see page 70).

2 Make a drawloop (see page 69) in what would normally be regarded as the long end of the line.

3 Pull tight in the direction of the arrows.

Alpine Butterfly or Linesman Loop

- When you want to make secure loops along a piece of rope, this is the knot you need. It is easy to tie, and it will not slip, whichever way you pull.

- Climbers use the Alpine butterfly to tie themselves together at safe intervals.

- You can make a complete rope ladder with this knot — use the loops as handholds and footholds.

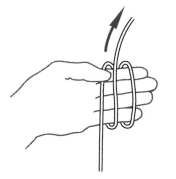 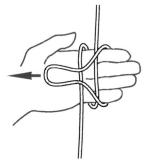 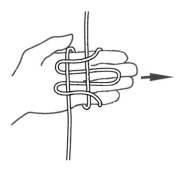

1 Holding it with your left thumb, coil the rope around your hand three times, laying the third loop between the first and second.

2 Gently pull the second coil over the other two.

3 Pull the second coil back under the other two, pulling out as much loop as you need.

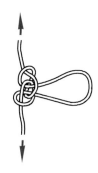 

4 Pull the loop and both ends to tighten the knot.

5 Make sure that it is tight but that the loop is big enough for your foot or hand.

Handcuff Knot

- Harry Houdini was the world's most famous escapologist, but according to legend this knot held him helpless. However, this is clearly nonsense, since there is nothing to prevent him from pulling his hands out.

- To make the knot secure you will need to tie the loose ends together with something like a square knot (see page 74). Then you could use it to handcuff a burglar or hobble a horse.

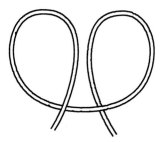

1 Make two identical loops in your rope — left over right, left over right.

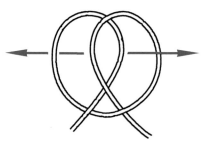

2 Pass the back loop in front of the front loop, as if to tie a clove hitch (see page 82).

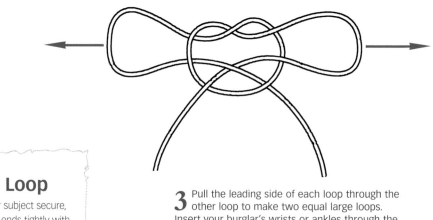

In the Loop

To keep your subject secure, tie the loose ends tightly with a square knot (see page 74).

3 Pull the leading side of each loop through the other loop to make two equal large loops. Insert your burglar's wrists or ankles through the loops, and then pull the ends tight, making sure that the center part of the knot is not loose.

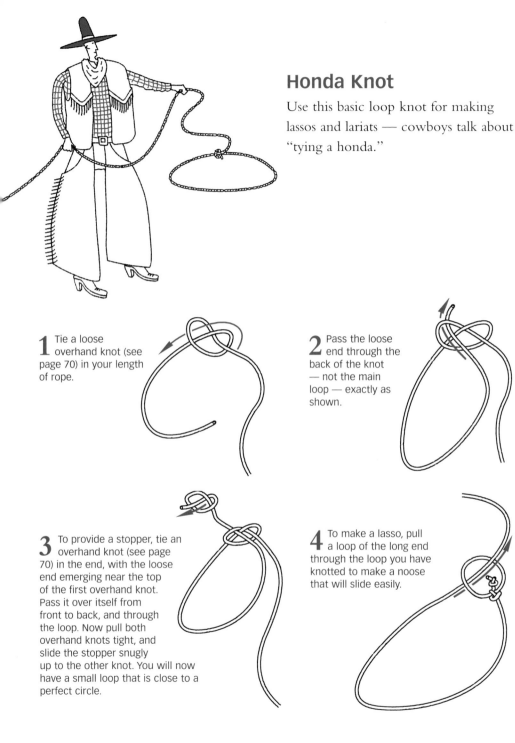

Honda Knot

Use this basic loop knot for making lassos and lariats — cowboys talk about "tying a honda."

1 Tie a loose overhand knot (see page 70) in your length of rope.

2 Pass the loose end through the back of the knot — not the main loop — exactly as shown.

3 To provide a stopper, tie an overhand knot (see page 70) in the end, with the loose end emerging near the top of the first overhand knot. Pass it over itself from front to back, and through the loop. Now pull both overhand knots tight, and slide the stopper snugly up to the other knot. You will now have a small loop that is close to a perfect circle.

4 To make a lasso, pull a loop of the long end through the loop you have knotted to make a noose that will slide easily.

Bowline and Running Bowline

- An extremely useful knot, the bowline is a loop that will not slip or jam.

- You can use a bowline knot to tether dogs and boats — just drop the loop over the post.

- Another use for this knot is to make a sling you can sit in or pass around the chest of a person who needs to be rescued.

In the Loop

To make a running bowline, pull the long end through the loop. This forms a noose that slides easily, but it is secure even when heavily loaded.

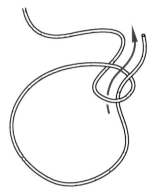

1 You need a long loose end to make your finished large loop, so start well up your rope.

2 Make a small loop above the larger loop.

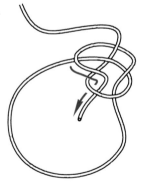

3 Feed the loose end up through the small loop, behind the long end, and then back down through the small loop.

4 Pull both long and loose ends to tighten the knot. The loose end should be inside the big loop.

Hangman's Knot

- Also known as the hangman's noose, this knot has ancient origins. It was commonly used from the sixteenth to the eighteenth centuries in capital punishment.

- The knot normally consists of 6–8 coils, depending on the friction required to cause death. According to superstition, the hangman's noose should have 13 coils, but this would render it useless.

- You can use the knot to secure rope to an eyelet or ring, or to weight a rope, making it easier to throw.

1 On a flat surface, use a long length of rope to create a large loop, with a smaller loop above it.

2 Coil the loose end around the three parallel lengths of rope, starting at the top of the lower loop. Coil it 6–8 times around the three ropes tightly in a clockwise direction.

3 Feed the loose end through the small loop at the top of the knot and pull it tight. The coil will now slide easily up and down the long end, opening and closing the loop below.

Whippings

The ends of a rope often fray, and become unraveled. This looks untidy, and it also makes the rope more difficult to use. Modern synthetic ropes are made of materials such as nylon, polyester, or polypropylene. The easiest way to stop these ropes from fraying is to melt the ends. Use a lighted match or lighter, and gently heat the end of the rope until you see the separate fibers soften and stick together.

Old-fashioned ropes are made from natural fibers, such as hemp, manila, or sisal.

Bringing up a flame to this type of rope will set fire to it, but will not seal the end. You can stop natural ropes from fraying by covering them with tape or by applying a blob of white glue, but the best way to stabilize the ends of these ropes is by whipping. This means binding the end tightly with thin string called whipping twine.

Note that for any type of whipping you need a long piece of whipping twine — about 10 feet (3 m) long for a rope that is around one inch (2.5 cm) thick.

Common Whipping

This is the simplest form of whipping that really works, and it is a good way to tidy the end of a rope without needing any special tools.

1 Lay a loop of twine along the rope, with the loose end 6 inches (15 cm) from the rope's end for a rope 1 inch (2.5 cm) thick, and the loop itself at the end. You may loop it around the end of one of the strands to keep it in place.

2 Tightly wind the long end around the rope, trapping both ends of the loop, starting about 2 inches (5 cm) from the end. Continue winding the twine tightly around, working toward the end of the rope, keeping each new turn tightly up against the previous one.

3 When you have covered 1 inch (2.5 cm) or 1.5 times the diameter of the rope, slip the end you are working with through the end of the loop you made in step 1, keeping the binding tight.

4 Pull the loose end of the loop hard to trap the long end, and then continue to pull carefully, until the loops lie under the center of the whipping. Cut both ends off as short as possible.

West Country Whipping

- Although it is likely to be more secure than a common whipping, this version is slow and tedious, and the final knot can come undone. However, it is a good whipping to use for thick ropes.

- Unlike the common and sailmaker's whippings, you work this one from the end of the rope inward, which makes it tricky to do.

1 In the middle of 10 feet (3 m) of whipping twine, tie a half hitch (see page 82), left over right, around the rope, half an inch from the end.

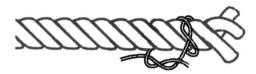

2 Turn the rope over and tie another half hitch, left over right, tight against the first turn, further from the end of the rope.

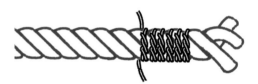

3 Repeat this process — turning the rope and tying a half hitch (see page 82) tightly against the last one — until you have covered a distance equal to 1½ times the diameter of the rope.

4 Instead of a half hitch, finish off by tying a square knot (see page 74).

Sailmaker's Whipping

- This is the most secure form of whipping you can do without a needle or stitching. It looks tricky but it is not difficult, and it looks professional.

- Sailors use this whipping to prevent the ends of three-core ropes from fraying, and to keep them tidy enough to pass easily through eyelets in sails.

1 Unravel the three strands at the end of the rope for about twice the diameter of the rope — 2 inches (5 cm) for a 1-inch (2.5 cm) rope. Using whipping twine — you will need about 10 feet (3 m) — make a loop between the strands of the rope so that it straddles one strand. The loop will stick out 3 inches (7.5 cm) on one side, and the loose end (A) 6 inches (15 cm) on the other.

2 Twist the three strands of rope together again. Holding the loop and the loose end (A) with the long end of the rope in your left hand, wind the twine tightly around the rope, working toward the end of the rope, and keeping successive turns tightly together. Continue winding until you have covered a distance equal to 1½ times the diameter of the rope.

3 While holding the whipping firmly, pick up the loop in the twine, and pass it over the end of the strand which it straddled, so that the sides of the loop follow the grooves between the strands. Pull the loose end (A) of the whipping to tighten the loop and trap both the loose end (B) and the whipping.

4 Take the loose end (A) — there will be only one free — along its groove to the end of the rope, and tie it tightly to the other end (B) in a square knot (see page 74) so that the square knot is buried in the center of the rope.

5 Trim the ends of the twine fairly short.

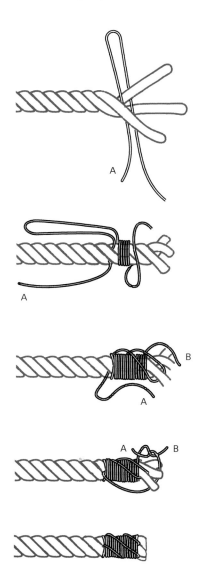

Shoelacing

Tying shoelaces is simple, isn't it? All you need to decide is what sort of knot to tie. Wrong. It is incredibly complicated, because there are so many different ways to do it. The average shoe has six eyelets on each side.

According to Australian mathematician Buckard Polster, if you want to easily lace up your shoes and have the two sides pulled together, there are about 43,000 ways to do it. When you tie the laces on both shoes, there are 43,000 x 43,000 = 1,849,000,000 or nearly two billion ways to do it.

Suppose you just put the laces wherever you please? Then as long as you use every eyelet once only, there are close to a trillion, trillion ways to tie your laces. That means that if the entire population of the world were tying shoelaces, and each tie took five minutes, and no two people ever came up with the same pattern, then it would take 1,525,798,664 years to tie every combination, which is more than 300 times as long as people have existed.

How do you get this huge number? With any of the 12 eyelets, you can go down or up; so that makes 24 ways. Then you go to any of the other 11 eyelets, and go down or up, which makes 24 x 22. In total, the number of lacing ways for one shoe is 24 x 22 x 20 x 18 x 16 x 14...x 4 x 2 divided by 2, because for each finished result you may have started at either end.

Crisscross Lacing

The crisscross is the simplest and most comfortable lacing. Master this before you try the other lacings in this section.

1 Push the end of the lace down through one of the bottom eyelets and up through the other. Pull the ends to the same length.

2 Take each end diagonally across to come up through the next eyelet on the other side.

3 Repeat step 2 until the laces are out through the top eyelets.

4 Tie in a bow.

In the Loop

For some reason, the natural way to tie shoelaces is with a granny knot (see page 75) bow, as shown here. This means that the ends of the bow will lie roughly up toward your ankle and down the shoe. It is much better to tie a square knot (see page 74), which is less likely to slip and easier to untie.

American Straight or Fashion Lacing

This technique is arguably more elegant than the European version, since there are no diagonals. This lacing also needs shorter laces than crisscross. However, there is a catch — it doesn't work if you have an odd number of eyelets.

1 Push the ends of the lace down through both bottom eyelets and pull them to the same length.

2 Take the right lace straight up, up through the second right eyelet, straight across, and down through the second left eyelet.

3 Take the left lace straight up, up through the third left eyelet, straight across, and down through the third right eyelet.

4 Carry on leapfrogging like this until you can take both laces out of the top eyelets and tie in a bow.

European Straight or Ladder Lacing

Many Europeans use this lacing for dress shoes. It looks particularly good if the gap between the eyelets is narrow, because all of the messy crossing happens underneath.

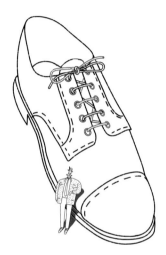

1 Poke the ends of the lace down through the bottom eyelets and pull them to the same length.

2 Take the left lace diagonally across and push it up through the second right eyelet, straight across, and down through the second left eyelet.

3 Take the right lace diagonally up, out through the third left eyelet, straight across, and down through the third right eyelet.

4 Continue with alternate laces until both can come out at the top. Tie in a bow.

Checkerboard Lacing

Sneakers with a wide front look very good with this lacing. You will need two pairs of laces with contrasting colors — black and white, for example.

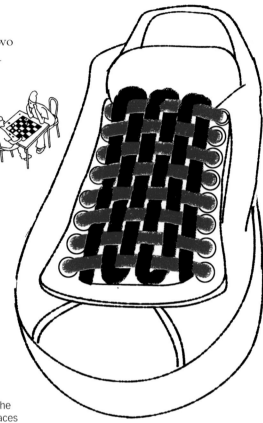

1 Push the end of the first color lace down though a bottom eyelet and straight up to the top, leaving the end 3 or 4 inches (7 or 8 cm) long.

2 Take the other end down through the other bottom eyelet, up to the next, straight across, and down through the next eyelet.

3 Continue doing this — straight up and up through the eyelet, straight across, and down, until you get to the top.

4 When you have gone down through the second top eyelet, tie the ends together in a bow underneath — this is tricky but not too difficult.

5 Take the other color lace and, starting at the bottom, weave it in and out of the cross laces until you get to the top.

6 Take it around the top lace, and then in and out all the way down again and around the bottom one. Push the two weaves close together.

7 Continue doing this until you have run out of space or lace. Then carefully tuck the ends out of sight.

Lattice Lacing

This is a cool method for tying sneakers, or boots.

1 Push one end of the lace down through one of the bottom eyelets and up through the other. Pull both ends to the same length.

2 Take both ends diagonally across and down through the fourth eyelets on the other side — skipping over two pairs on each side.

3 Take both ends straight up and through the fifth eyelets, then diagonally down and across and down through the second eyelets — again skipping over two pairs.

4 Go straight up and up through the third pair of eyelets, then diagonally up to the sixth pair.

5 If this is the top pair, go up through them and tie in a bow. If there is a seventh pair, go down through the sixth, straight up, go up through the seventh, and tie.

Bow Tie Lacing

An elegant hybrid of the crisscross and straight versions, this lacing is very economical in lace length.

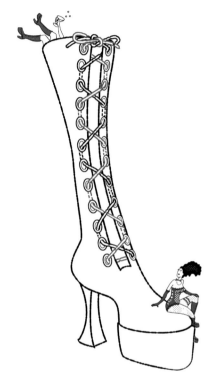

1 Bring the lace up through the bottom eyelets and pull to equal length.

2 Cross over diagonally, down through the second eyelets, straight up, and up through the third.

3 Repeat this process until you come out at the top, and tie in a bow.

Ladder Lacing

A tricky lacing to do, it uses a lot of lace — so it is a good one to use if your laces are too long. It also can be made really tight, so it is good for ice skates and hiking boots.

1 Bring up both ends through the bottom eyelets and pull to equal length.

2 Take both ends straight up, and down into the next eyelets.

3 Take each end across, under the vertical lace on the other side, straight up, and down through the next eyelet.

4 Repeat this process until you get to the top, where you go down through the top eyelets, across and underneath, and then tie the ends in a bow.

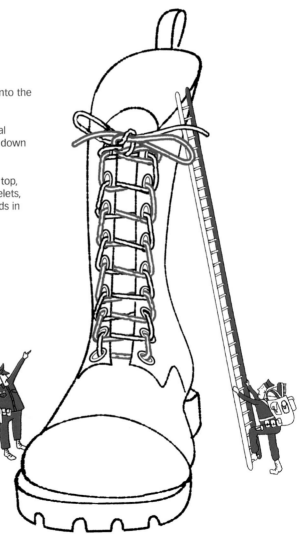

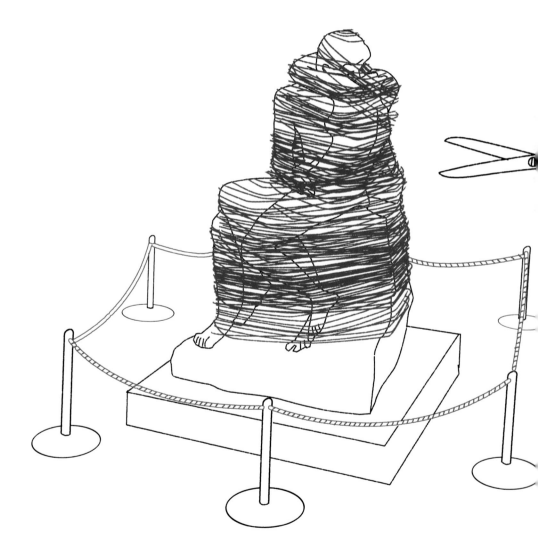

The Art
of String

We've already seen how practical string and its cousins rope and yarn can be. Now let's have a look at their role in the arts and leisure. From ancient myths to action films, musical instruments to architectural models, magic tricks to puppetry, and archery to rappelling, they have myriad uses.

Cultured String

From music to architecture, and crafts to poetry, string and rope are an essential part of our cultural lives.

String in the Arts

Physical string and rope are used in instruments to help create notes, they are manipulated in puppets to help them move, and they are employed to craft things from bookbindings to macramé potholders.

String is also a powerful metaphor and inspiration in everything, from everyday expressions to poetry.

Instrument String Musical strings used for violins, guitars, and all types of other stringed instruments (see pages 110-112) were originally made of catgut (actually sheep's intestines),

which were stretched, dried, and twisted. Modern strings are made of either steel (especially the top E-string on a violin) or nylon, and the heavier strings — used to produce lower notes — are wound with metal wires.

Craft String Knitters and crocheters mainly use wool or cotton yarn for their projects, although a few things, such as scrubbing cloths and string net bags are often made from household string. For crafts, such as macramé, you can use most types of string — the basic cotton household sort, hemp garden twine, or even linen bookbinding thread. However, you will find a good range of craft string in craft stores, which give you a wider choice of colors than the regular varieties. Most craft stores also stock the brightly colored plastic string often used for making friendship bracelets (see page 58). This plastic lacing is also known as gimp, boondoggle, lanyard, or scooby-doo. You also are likely to find paper string or twine. This is usually used for tying gifts, or for paper crafts, such as scrapbooking.

Bookbinding String Books don't escape the need for string. Many art bookbinders use fine linen string or thread to stitch together their hand-made bindings by using one of several traditional methods to create a beautiful finish.

Some handstitched bindings are deliberately left on display, rather than hidden inside a spine. These types are worked in subtly colored — often hand-dyed — linen string for effect. In such cases the string is chosen or custom-made in order to complement the other high quality materials being used to make the book — handmade papers, tooled leather, gold leaf, and special inks.

You may not actually own one of these works of bookbinding art, but some of the books on your shelf may still have bindings

stitched with thread or string. This is because the pages of the better quality mass-produced hardbacks are stitched together along the spine by machine before being glued into the hardback cover, rather than simply glued to the spine backing.

Goje
(West Africa)

Requinto
(Mexico)

Double Bass
(Europe)

Tromba
Marina
(Europe)

Matouqin
(Mongolia)

Piano
(Europe)

Dotar
(Central Asia)

Sitar
(India)

Balalaika
(Eastern Europe)

Hammered Dulcimer
(Europe and Asia)

Global Orchestra There
are hundreds of stringed
instruments in play around
the world — from the Western
classical quartet of violin,
double bass, and piano, to more
unusual instruments used in
regional folk music.

Music and Strings

The earliest stringed instrument may have originated when a hunter plucked the string of his bow and unwittingly invented the harp. The oldest documented references are from 3000 BCE in Mesopotamia and Egypt. The Old Testament of the Bible mentions King David playing a harplike instrument.

Oud
(Middle East
and Northern
Africa)

Koto
(Japan)

Hurdy Gurdy
(Europe)

Er-Hu
(China)

Pedal Steel Guitar
(North America)

A World of Strings Throughout the centuries, different cultures have developed all sorts of stringed instruments. The Middle Eastern oud was brought to the West by the Crusaders, and influenced the development of the lute. The oud has 11 strings, which were traditionally plucked with an eagle quill. In contrast, the Central Asian dotar has only two strings (dotar is Persian for two strings), as does the Chinese er-hu, which is played with a rosined bow that is worked between its pair of strings. The Mongolian matouquin, another stringed instrument, has strings made from horsetail hair, and it is topped by a carved headstock, often depicting a horse.

How Does a Stringed Instrument Work? Stringed instruments make their sound by being plucked, hit, or bowed. Those that are plucked include the harp, guitar, harpsichord, and the violin family, although the violin and its larger siblings — viola, double bass, and cello — are more commonly bowed. In jazz, however, the double bass is usually plucked. Piano strings are struck by hammers.

Violins, acoustic guitars, and other related instruments use a hollow body to improve the quality of the note — not to amplify the vibration produced by the strings, but to use the greater surface area to provide better coupling with the air. These instruments are traditionally made from wood, especially spruce or maple. However, instruments are now being made from fiberglass and carbon fiber.

Violins The best-known stringed instrument in Western classical music is the violin, also informally known as the fiddle, which first appeared around 1600. The finest violin maker of all time is the Italian Antonio Stradivari (1644–1737). A violin repairer (luthier) in London recently handed me a Stradivarius, saying casually, "This is a midrange instrument — only worth about three million dollars." I handed it back very quickly.

Guitars The favorite stringed instrument in popular music is the guitar, which originated in Spain. It is good for accompanying singers because it is fairly quiet. In the 1930s people began to electronically amplify guitars to enable them to be heard in dance bands, and the electric guitar became the mainstay of rock bands.

Architectural Strings

The architectural uses of rope and string are not just confined to bell ropes. More than a hundred years ago the innovative Catalan architect Antoni Gaudí used string to create models of his extraordinary buildings. He first tried this out in 1898, in his design for a church at Santa Coloma de Cervello, near Barcelona, Spain. He made a string model to represent the structural ribs of the building. Next he hung weights from the strings, which were proportional to the loads they were to bear. This created a representation of the vaulting structure, ensuring that it could be supported without buttresses. The amazing thing was that the entire string model was upside down. Gaudí photographed it from every angle, and then turned the photographs over to make plans for the actual building. The tension in each string became compression in the fabric of the building.

Making a Model with String

The architecture school at the Massachusetts Institute of Technology (MIT) offers a workshop based on a virtual version of Gaudí's string modeling method. Designers can work on a computer and interact with the program by cutting virtual strings and adding virtual weights to see how their building changes form in three dimensions. More simply, you can make a physical model of a dome by draping string soaked in white glue over a balloon. Once it is dry, puncture the balloon to leave behind a curved framework.

Stringy Folk Tales

Several intriguing stories involving string and rope are woven through international folklore. Here are a few of the best examples.

Native American Blue-Sky Thinking

According to the legend of the Cherokee tribe, every creature lived in the sky except for one, Dayunsi, a water beetle who lived in the sea. There was overcrowding in the sky, and the animals were crying out for more space, so the mighty Dayunsi swam down to the bottom of the ocean, which was covered in mud. He came back up to tell everyone of his discovery, and The Creator, or Powerful One, gave him four thick strings, which he then attached to the four corners of the mud seabed. All of the animals in the sky heaved and hauled the bottom of the sea up to the surface. When it dried, all of the animals came down from the sky to live on the ground, and so the Earth was created.

An African Tale There are many stories of the human fall from grace. The river people of Sudan believed that there was a rope tied between Earth and heaven. However, one day a hyena chewed through the rope and so angered the gods that they made people mortal, and brought death to the Earth. The hyena has been resented ever since.

Chinese Connections In Chinese mythology, the great Yuelao and his assistant gods were in the habit of tying an invisible red string around the ankles of couples destined to be soul mates. This thread shackled the lovers regardless of time or space. It could twist and tangle, but it could never break. This might explain why some couples stick together even through very rocky relationships.

Egyptian Knots and Amulets The ancient Egyptians believed that knots could retain magical powers, so they were frequently used in amulets. There was a symbol and a hieroglyph for the "Knot of Isis," which was similar to the knots securing the robes of the god. It was supposed to symbolize the blood flow from Isis's womb, but the knot is actually much older than Isis herself.

Greek Classics

So much of our culture was invented by the ancient Greeks — politics, music, theater, philosophy, mathematics — that it is hardly surprising that much of Greek mythology is tied up with string. Or perhaps it would be more accurate to say that the reason we are so enmeshed in string culture today is because we inherited the idea of using string from those clever old Greeks.

Ariadne's Thread Following his victory in battle with the Athenians, the king of Crete demanded that seven Athenian youths be sent as sacrificial victims to the Minotaur, a beast that was half man, half bull. Theseus, king of Athens, took the place of one of the victims, and vowed to find his way through the labyrinth — a vast maze made of rock — and kill the Minotaur. He managed the task with the help of Ariadne, the daughter of the king of Crete, who gave him a huge ball of red thread. He tied the end at the entrance of the labyrinth, and unwound the thread as he cautiously felt his way through. He knew if he followed the thread on the ground, he could find his way out again. He managed to kill the Minotaur, find his way out, and run away with Ariadne.

Dionysus Unbound Meanwhile, in another Greek myth, the young Dionysus, the god of wine, was about to be kidnapped by sailors. However, when they tried to tie him up, they found that no rope could bind him — and then he turned into a lion.

Arachne's Web Arachne, a young girl from Lydia, was so skilled at weaving that people said she must have been trained by Athena, the goddess of weaving, herself. Over time, the praise went to Arachne's head, and she came to believe that she was better than the goddess. Angered at this mere mortal's audacity, Athena challenged her to a weaving contest. It has never been clear whose work was the best, but the story goes that Athena, shocked both by the flawlessness of her rival Arachne's work and its subject matter — she chose to tell the stories of indiscretions committed by the gods in her weaving — smashed her loom and tore the tapestry to shreds. She touched Arachne on the forehead to make sure that she felt guilty for her actions. The young girl's shame was so intense that she hanged herself. Athena took pity on her, loosened the rope, which she changed into a thread, and brought her back to life as a spider. From then on, Arachne and her descendants were destined literally to hang by a thread, and to be great weavers.

The Rope of Oknos In Greek mythology, the rope of Oknos is a metaphor for pointless work. Rather like poor Sisyphus who spent his days rolling heavy stones uphill, only to see them rolling down again every night, Oknos spent his days weaving a rope that was eaten by a donkey as fast as he made it. Oknos was condemned to Hades, but he remains the patron saint of researchers and graduate students.

Knotty Problem The Gordian knot could not be undone, so Alexander's clever solution to cut it free was definitely a master stroke.

The Gordian Knot

The city of Gordium in Phrygia (now northwest Turkey) was founded, according to legend, by King Gordias in the ninth century BCE He — or possibly his son, Midas — tied the immensely intricate Gordian knot and used it to tie a cart to a pole. The knot was so complicated that it seemed to be impossible to untie, and an oracle predicted that whoever could solve the problem would become king of Asia.

Alexander the Great visited Gordium in 333 BCE and wrestled with the knot for some time, but he found that he could not untie it. So he drew his sword and with one mighty stroke, cut right through it. He went on to conquer Asia, fulfilling the prophecy. As a result, "to cut the Gordian knot" has become a metaphor for solving a difficult problem with a bold stroke.

Bookish Yarns

Over the centuries and around the world, writers have spun yarns around string. In her novel *The Shipping News*, American novelist Annie Proulx named her chief protagonist Quoyle, after an old term for a coil of rope. She opened each chapter with knotty references — many quoted from the classic *The Ashley Book of Knots*.

Stringy Quotes Stringy references appear in many timeless works. Here are a few of the more well-known quotes.

"Egypt, thou knew'st too well, My heart was to thy rudder tied by th' strings, And thou shouldst tow me after..."
— William Shakespeare, *Antony and Cleopatra*

"I am an overstrained string that must snap. But it's not ended yet... and it will have a fearful end."
— Leo Tolstoy, *Anna Karenina*

"I give you the end of a golden string, Only wind it into a ball; It will lead you in at Heaven's gate, Built in Jerusalem's wall."
— William Blake, *Jerusalem*

De Maupassant's Story The nineteenth century French writer Guy de Maupassant wrote a short story called *La Ficelle* (*A Piece of String*). To sum up the plot: One market day in a small town, Maitre Hauchecorne was walking toward the main square when he saw a little piece of string on the ground. He picked it up, but was seen bending down by someone he had fallen out with. He felt embarrassed about seeming so penny-pinching, so he pretended that he was looking for something he had dropped. Later that day, it transpired that a billfold was lost at that very spot and Maitre

The Smoked Herring

"Once upon a time there was a big white wall — bare, bare, bare,
 Against the wall there stood a ladder — high, high, high,
 And on the ground a smoked herring — dry, dry, dry,
He comes, holding in his hands — dirty, dirty, dirty,
 A heavy hammer and a big nail — sharp, sharp, sharp,
 A ball of string — big, big, big,
Then he climbs the ladder — high, high, high,
 And drives the sharp nail — tock, tock, tock,
 Way up on the big white wall — bare, bare, bare,
He drops the hammer — down, down, down,
 To the nail he fastens a string — long, long, long,
 And, at the end, the smoked herring — dry, dry, dry,
He comes down the ladder — high, high, high,
 He picks up the hammer — heavy, heavy, heavy,
 And goes off somewhere — far, far, far,
And ever afterwards the smoked herring — dry, dry, dry,
 At the end of that string — long, long, long,
 Very slowly sways — forever and ever and ever.
I made up this story — silly, silly, silly,
 To infuriate the squares — solemn, solemn, solemn,
 And to amuse the children — little, little, little."

— *Charles Cros, nineteenth-century French poet and inventor*

Hauchecorne's enemy reported seeing him pick it up. Challenged
by the police, he protested his innocence and explained that he
was just picking up a piece of string. Although he pulled the string
out of his pocket, no one believed him. The next day, the missing
billfold was found and handed in. But people still suspected Maitre
Hauchecorne of stringing them along, and he was ribbed about
the incident frequently. He obsessed about proving his innocence,
making himself ill. On his deathbed, he still protested: "A little bit
of string. A little bit of string. See, here it is Monsieur le Maire."

Crafty String

There are so many artful ways of using string that hundreds of books have been written about it. Here is a taste of what you can do if you feel artistic and have a ball of string or wool, or a piece of rope.

Teased Collage Take a piece of rope, perhaps 6 inches (15 cm) long. Unwind one end, then unwind some of the strands and some of the thin stringy pieces. Lay all of it on a piece of black card stock on which you have smeared white woodwork glue — and put a weight on top (perhaps a book, on top of a piece of newspaper). Leave it to dry. Remove the weight, and you have made a collage.

Knitting My mother used to knit. My sister used to knit. My brother used to knit. Even I used to knit, although I always had to concentrate hard to avoid dropping stitches. In practice, knitting is just a way of turning knots into a warm sheet of wool. A knitted sweater is usually made of four complicated knots: one each for the front and back, and one each for the sleeves.

Macramé Often used for wall hangings and to support suspended flower pots, macramé can be as simple or as complicated as you wish. To get a taste of the craft, take a long piece of kitchen string, tie the middle with a cow hitch (see page 83) to a suitable support, such as the back of a chair, or the handle of a drawer. Then use one long end to tie repeated half hitches (see page 82) around the other, making a spiral pattern.

String and Pins I have a picture on my wall of a tall ship in full sail on a blue ocean. It is made entirely of wool, which is stretched between pins in the baseboard. Making pictures like this from yarn or string was a popular craft in the 1960s and '70s.

Arty String

Both string and rope are wonderfully flexible
and easy to use. And in most cases
whatever you do, you can also undo.
So they lend themselves to all sorts
of experimental art: not only
pictures and sculptures, but
also elaborate installations.

One of the pioneers
of modern art was Marcel
Duchamp. In 1942, Duchamp draped an entire
gallery in New York with string and entitled it *Sixteen Miles of
String*. In 2006, Canadian artist Angela Bulloch paid homage to
Duchamp at the Tate Modern in London, England, by creating an
intricate web of string, dangling from the ceiling to the floor.

Sculptor Barbara Hepworth used string in many of her works,
including *Pelagos*. Inspired by a coastal bay, this piece consists of a
hollowed-out wooden spiral, painted on the inside and with string
tensioned across it. Hepworth said that the string expresses "the
tension felt between myself and the sea, the wind or the hills."

At the Tate Modern in 2003, English sculptor and installation
artist Cornelia Parker transformed Auguste Rodin's famous
sculpture *The Kiss* by wrapping it in a mile of string to represent
the claustrophobia that can arise in a relationship. She called it *The
Distance: A Kiss with String Attached*. A protester was horrified at
her work and the "mutilation" of Rodin's art, and he attacked the
string wrapping with a pair of scissors.

In the late 1990s, the artist Christo, with a team of several
hundred helpers, spent six days wrapping an entire building in
80 acres (32 hectares) of silvery plastic film, tied up with 5 miles
(8 km) of blue string binding.

Rope at the Circus

Ropes over a three-ring circus can hold up the big top tent, suspend the trapeze, form the tightrope, and much more.

Big Top Ropes The first circus owner to house his performance in a large canvas tent was Joshua Purdy Brown in Wilmington, Delaware, in 1825. Before long, the big top was an essential, central part of any circus. Like all old-fashioned tents, big tops were made of canvas supported on poles and held down at the corners and edges by guy ropes. Circus ropes have some special terminology:

- **Tunny ropes** help to support the canvas.
- **Spanish webs** are long cloth-covered ropes on which acrobats perform by spinning horizontally.
- **To rag out** is to tighten the tent ropes.

Tightrope Walking The ancient Greeks were tightrope walkers. Since then, the tightrope or high wire has been a popular circus act. The "rope" in a tightrope is sometimes rope, but more often it is a steel wire. Professionals use thin slippers when walking on wire and bare feet on rope. The stunts have different names:

- **High wire** is at least 23 feet (7 m) above the ground.
- **Sky walking** takes place outdoors over a considerable distance.
- **Tightwire** is a tensioned wire.
- **Slack wire** is a loose wire that is kept in tension by only the walker's weight.

Starting in 1859, French acrobat Blondin walked over Niagara Falls 17 times. His rope — and it probably was a rope, since steel cable would have been impossibly heavy — was 1,100 feet (335 m) long, and 160 feet (48 m) above the water. On one occasion he carried his manager across, and almost fell off the rope.

Theatrical Ropes

The ancient Greeks were the pioneers of theater as we know it, and many Greek plays are still performed today. In some of these plays, actors were suspended on ropes to give the illusion that they were flying.

The Fly System The seventeenth century saw the advent of the proscenium arch, or "pros arch," which stands over the front of the stage. It allows curtains to be pulled across to signify the end of an act and hides the shifting of scenery. The pros arch also allows for the installation of various mechanisms above the stage and out of sight of the audience, including the fly system.

The fly system is the network of ropes and pulleys that allows sets, props, microphones, and people to be lowered on ropes from the fly space, tower, or gallery. The flying is controlled from a gallery at the side of the stage called the fly floor. The ropes go up from here to pulleys in the grid at the top of the fly tower, and from the tower down to the stage. In a big theater there may be as many as 50 sets of ropes, which are capable of lifting things 70 feet (20 m) above the stage.

The process of lowering something onto the stage is called hemp flying. Therefore, theaters are sometimes called hemp houses, because hemp ropes were traditionally used, although sisal is often used instead. In modern theaters steel wire is common, and there are generally counterweights to balance the loads, as well as electric motors to fly the actors across the stage. Hemp fly systems are still in use today because they are less expensive than the steel versions and easier to install. However, they are harder to operate and demand more muscle power. Because the rope work is similar to that found on ships, former sailors have often been employed as hemp flymen.

Magic with String

Here are two magic tricks you can use to baffle your friends and neighbors. Make sure that you practice thoroughly to perfect the magic before you try it out on anyone — there is nothing as disappointing as a badly done trick.

Air Knot This trick is easier to undertake with soft, slippery rope. You will need a piece 20 inches (50 cm) long. You do the whole thing with one hand, so make sure that you use your better hand — right if you are right-handed or left if left-handed.

1 Challenge your audience to throw a piece of rope in the air so that it comes down with a knot in it. Show them the rope, and let them try it a few times. Say that you can do it, as long as you say the magic word. Hold your hand palm up, and hold the rope between the last two fingers, with about 6 inches (15 cm) below your hand. The rest will cross your palm and hang down between first finger and thumb.

YOU NEED TO DO THE FOLLOWING STEPS SMOOTHLY AND FAIRLY QUICKLY, WITH ONE FLUID MOVEMENT:

2 Rotate your hand, thumb over and down, making sure that the end that was by your thumb swings nearer to you than the end that is by your pinkie. As your hand becomes palm down, bend your wrist and grab the loose end of the rope between your first and second fingers. There should be about 2 inches (5 cm) of loose end sticking out.

3 Say the magic word "ABRASTRINGABRA," and as you say it, toss the rope into the air with an energetic flourish, keeping hold with first and second fingers until the last moment. If you get it right, the rope will come down with a simple overhand knot in it. Show it to your audience so they can see that it is real, and challenge them to do it, too.

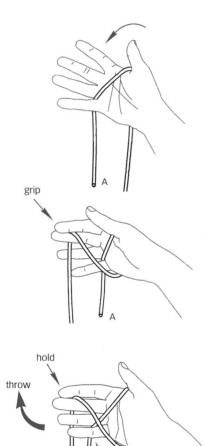

grip

A

hold

throw

let go

Cut and Mend This trick is easier (and cheaper) if you use string rather than rope. You need about 3 feet (1 m) of string and a pair of scissors.

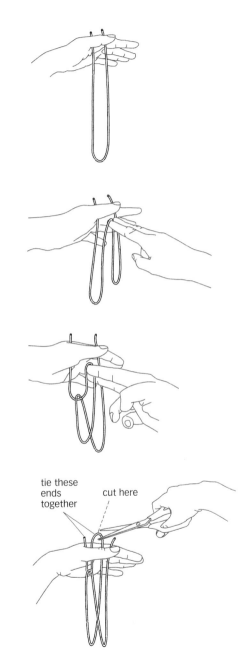

1 Hold your left-hand palm toward you, with both ends of the string held by your thumb and in view. Be sure to keep the loop they form hidden behind your hand. Tell your audience that you are going to cut the string in half, then miraculously mend it again.

2 Pick up the middle of the loop of string with first finger and thumb and bring it up behind your hand. As your right hand comes up behind your left — while hidden from your audience — let go with your thumb so that the loop hangs on your first finger.

3 Then, with your second finger, smoothly and quickly hook the left end of the string just below your thumb, and grab this new loop with finger and thumb (dropping the old one) before showing it over the top of your left hand. Hold all four strings in your left finger and thumb.

4 Produce the scissors, and cut the new loop yourself. Announce that you are going to tie the ends together again, and tie the two left-hand ends with an overhand knot (see page 70). The knot you form actually ties the short end to the middle of the main piece of string. Hold up the string by both ends, and ask your audience to agree that you have two pieces of string tied together. Then say the magic word: "ABRASTRINGABRA." Next, while holding one end tight, slide your other hand quicky along the string, sliding off the short end you have tied around it. Casually slip the short end into your pocket, throw the other piece to the audience, and ask them to find the join.

tie these ends together   cut here

Marionettes

Puppets controlled by strings are called marionettes. They are more difficult to use than glove, finger, chinface, and body puppets (in which the operator is inside the figure of the puppet — think Mickey Mouse), and learning to operate them well takes a long time. The operators are out of sight, and the strings are usually black so that they are hard to see, allowing the audience to enter into the illusion that the puppets move about on their own.

Puppet History Marionettes have been used in theater for thousands of years. String puppets made of clay and ivory have been found in the tombs of ancient Egypt; they were probably used in rituals and ceremonies. The Greek mathematician Archimedes played with marionettes at his home in Sicily, and Plato wrote about them. Some have been found in Greek children's graves dating back to 500 BCE.

The Romans copied many things from the Greeks, and marionettes were among them. Modern marionettes seem to have evolved from Roman puppets, although the word marionette is French. It dates from around 1600, and means little Mary. Most likely, the term referred to the Virgin Mary, since the puppets were used in the Christian church during the Middle Ages for morality plays representing simple stories from the Bible. They were later banned by the Church, because they could so easily be used for mischievous satirical purposes.

By the eighteenth century, marionettes had become an important element of the entertainment industry. So much so that special theaters were built for them, and entire operas were written for performance by marionettes — even Joseph Haydn wrote one. Marionette operas are still performed at the Salzburg Theatre, Salzburg, Austria, the Schoenbeim Palace in Vienna, Austria, and the National Marionette Theatre in Prague, Czech Republic.

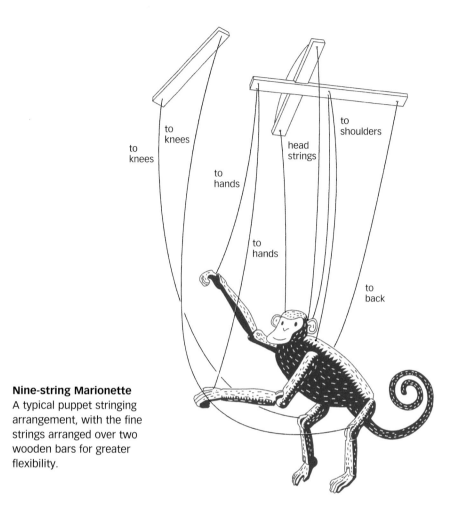

Nine-string Marionette
A typical puppet stringing arrangement, with the fine strings arranged over two wooden bars for greater flexibility.

Puppet on a String Today, there are two main forms of string puppet: Sicilian marionettes are basic, with a metal rod extending through the head and body and one hand operated by a single string. The Czech type are fully articulated and have multiple movements. For realistic movement, the hands, feet, and bottoms of the puppets are all weighted. The weight of the whole figure is carried on the head string, or the shoulder strings. A typical puppet has nine strings, attached to the head, shoulders, hands, legs, and feet, but some complex figures have as many as 30 strings to enable intricate movements.

The Indian Rope Trick

From the mysterious East in the nineteenth century came exotic tales of hot food, snake charmers, and strangest of all, the Indian rope trick. The story usually went something like this: After a good dinner in a palace, the guests would be called out onto a balcony to watch a magical performance. A fakir, or holy man, appeared with a large coil of rope. After chanting a strange incantation, he threw one end of the rope up into the air. Instead of falling down again, it climbed higher and stayed there swaying, as if tied to a hook in the dark sky above. A young boy ran up, dodged the fakir, and climbed nimbly up the rope until he disappeared into the sky above. The fakir called him down, and then, enraged, shook his fist, drew a large *kukhri* (knife) from his belt, and climbed up the rope. He also disappeared, but there were terrible screams from above, and bloody arms and legs came crashing down.

In some versions of the story the fakir climbed down and put all the body parts in a basket, and the boy reappeared from behind the crowd, begging for money.

What was going on? Levitation? Mass hallucination? Could it all be a hoax? Could there be a wire high up in the darkness and an assistant to catch the rope? According to Peter Lamont of Edinburgh University, the story was a hoax, invented by John Elbert Wilkie, who wrote for the *Chicago Herald Tribune* in 1890 under the pen name Fred S. Ellmore ("Sell more"), in order to boost the circulation of his newspaper. Four months later the newspaper admitted it was a hoax, but by then the story was out, and many people still believe it today.

String on Screen

You might think string plays a minor role in film, but so many movies feature string and rope in one way or another that a list would be as long as a piece of string. Perhaps it should start with the cheese-string finale to *Mousehunt* (1997), which has the punchline "A world without string is chaos."

Ropy Action Many Western movies seem to feature rope, whether it is used to lasso steers, tie up bad guys, or hang bandits. In *The Good, the Bad, and the Ugly* (1966) Blondie (Clint Eastwood) rescues the wanted bandit Tuco (Eli Wallach), turns him in for the reward money, and then shoots through the rope when Tuco is hanged from a tree. They share the proceeds and repeat the scam. Similarly, every epic adventure tale has people scaling mountains (*The Eiger Sanction*, 1975) or climbing up and down ropes to surprise their enemies. For example, in *The Guns of Navarone* (1961) the Allied commandos have to climb impossibly high cliffs.

You have probably seen James Bond scenes with rope — most notably the Japanese good guys rappeling into the fake volcano crater in *You Only Live Twice* (1967). More subtly, in the same movie, an assassin tries to murder Bond (played by Sean Connery) by dribbling poison down a string onto his face while he is asleep — but his poor bedfellow dies instead.

Probably the most dramatic use of ropes in film is in bridges, which are always cut or broken at one end at the critical moment. In his quest for the *Temple of Doom* (1984), Indiana Jones is stuck in the middle of a rope bridge with bad guys at both ends. He cuts the bridge himself to keep one lot away, but still (after crashing into the cliff) has to climb the other side and outwit the bandits with devilish cunning. Rope bridges also make an appearance in many other films, including *Cliffhanger* (1993), *Shrek* (2001), and *Kung Fu Panda* (2008).

Sporty String

From finely tensioned tennis rackets and archery bows to vital climbing equipment, there is an Olympic roster of sporting uses for string and rope.

Sporty Fibers

Common hemp fiber (see page 14) is usually used in the ropes that are employed in sports, such as tug-of-war and Japanese rope binding, as well as in theaters.

Today, high-tech ropes made from synthetic fibers are also popular, particularly for adventure sports, such as climbing, where safety considerations play a part. However, boxing prefers manila fiber for its ropes. Derived from the leaves of the plant *Musa texlis*, this tea-colored rope is as strong as hemp, but it is less prone to rot.

Here are some more descriptions of the strings and ropes that are used in different sports.

Tennis The origins of tennis lie in the ancient English game of royal tennis or real tennis, which was played by King Henry VIII and many other monarchs. It is still played in a few places, including Hampton Court, England, where I have been reduced to a sweaty heap by a former British champion.

Lawn tennis rackets were originally made of wood, and the strings were generally made of sheep gut, known in the trade as serosa. To string a whole racket takes two sheep, and because after World War II sheep became somewhat scarce, cow gut was used instead. In the 1960s nylon strings appeared. So you could choose between gut, which is expensive and arguably gives most power (but it goes soggy in damp conditions and may break), polyester, which is much more durable; or Kevlar, which is very stiff and very durable. Tight strings provide more control, while loose strings give more power.

Squash racket strings are similar to tennis racket strings. Badminton racket strings are thinner (about 0.7 mm) because a shuttlecock is much lighter than a tennis ball.

Gymnastic Ropework

A rhythmic discipline, which is performed only by women, ropework began in the nineteenth century as a form of dance, and it became a sport in Russia in the 1940s. When the gymnast stands on one end of the rope, the other end needs to reach up to her shoulders. The rope may be made of hemp or a synthetic fiber, or a ribbon can be used. The rope can be open or folded, held in one hand or both, generally with a knot at the end. It is then thrown, waved, or whirled, often in combination with jumps and leaps. Ropework displays flexibility, agility, and grace. It is also supposed to suggest emotions, such as anger when it wraps around a post.

Adventure Sports

You also can enjoy adrenalin-pumping adventures and risk your life at the end of a rope, in sports such as climbing, caving, rappelling, and bungee jumping.

Traditional climbing, rappelling, and caving ropes were made of hemp, but today's nylon and polyester ropes are lighter and stronger. Dynamic ropes, which stretch and absorb the impact of a fall, are better than static ropes. These do not stretch, and unfortunately give a horrific jerk, which is extremely uncomfortable for the jumper.

Jumping from a high building, bridge, or cliff on the end of an elastic cord, or bungee jumping, has become increasingly popular. Bungee rope consists of latex strands enclosed in a durable braided outer cover. To allow it to stretch, the cord must be substantially shorter than the height of the jumping point from the ground. When the cord reaches its natural length, the jumper slows down, accelerating upward, and bounces back up.

Fighting String and Rope

Throughout history, people have always wanted to fight successful battles against their enemies. Today, string and rope feature significantly in fighting sports, rather than military operations.

Tug-of-War Perhaps the simplest of all team rope contests, tug-of-war has been a competitive sport for at least 4,000 years. According to the rules of the Tug-of-War International Federation, teams should consist of eight people, and the rope should be 4–5 inches (10–12 cm) in circumference and at least 110 feet (33 m) long, without any knots or features that would provide a good grip, although the pullers may use rosin on their hands.

The center of the rope is indicated with a red mark, which is lined up with a mark on the ground. There are white marks 13 feet (4 m) on either side of the red mark, and blue marks 3 feet (1 m) beyond the white ones. The front person in each team must grip the rope outside but as close as possible to the blue mark. The

Highland Tug-of-War The sport is a feature of the Scottish Highland Games. Today, more of these events are held in America than in Scotland.

winner is the team that pulls its opponents' white mark past the mark on the ground. (Note that these exact colors are not required, but the tapes need to be different colors.)

Boxing on the Ropes Boxing rings are designed to contain the match and to prevent the contestants from hurtling out into the surrounding crowd. Although they are called rings, they are not circular but square, and they are generally between 16-24 feet (5-7 m) square. According to the World Boxing Authority, a boxing ring should have four ropes, spaced 18, 30, 42, and 54 inches (45, 76, 106 and 137 cm) above the ground. They need protective covers, and they can be made of any material except for metal. However, in practice, they are usually made of manila (see page 130), and are 1–inch (2.5 cm) thick.

The practice of boxing has given rise to several common ropy expressions, including "on the ropes," "up against the ropes," "he's in a corner now," and "he came out fighting."

Archery Back in 1139, the longbow was a military weapon, and it was very successfully used in battle, despite being banned by the Pope as being "deathly and hateful to God, and unfit to be used by Christians." For example, in 1415 British King Henry V's army of 6,000 longbowmen killed 15,000 French soldiers while losing only about 300 men.

The medieval longbow was a wooden pole, as long as a man was tall, and tapered at the ends, which were often tipped with horn for strength. The linen bowstring had loops at the ends to slip over the horn tips into grooves, and it was 6 inches (15 cm) shorter than the bow, which was bent into a gentle curve. The bow would have a draw weight of around 170 pounds (77 kg), and it was lethal at up to 650 feet (200 m), where an arrow would penetrate normal body armor. More recent versions were made of yew wood, but today's bows are made from synthetic laminates — sandwiches of

various polymeric materials — which gives them immense power and precision; they would have delighted Henry's archers. Modern bowstrings are generally made of synthetic material such as braided polyester. They can be simple or reverse-twisted — where individual bundles are twisted one way and the groups of these bundles are then twisted the other way to give extra strength.

Like most sports, archery has some particular names for its equipment. Here are a few basic terms used by the makers of bows:

- **A Flemish string** has a loop at one end to hook over the tip of the bow.
- **Looped strings** are made in continuous loops of material.
- **The serving** is the thickened part of the bowstring and the part that the archer holds.
- **The nook** is where the arrow goes.

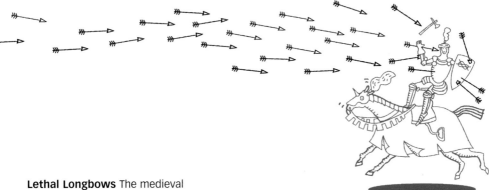

Lethal Longbows The medieval longbow helped the English archers to victory over the French Army at the Battle of Agincourt in 1415.

Hojojutsu: Japanese Rope Binding

A set of traditional Japanese martial art methods of restraining prisoners, Hojojutsu dates from the 1600s, and it is still taught to Japanese police today. The simplest form uses a single, ⅛ to ⅙ inch- (3-4 mm) thick cord called a hayanawa (fast rope), which the policeman would wrap around a suspect in a particular pattern. But he would not use knots, in order to avoid bringing shame to the prisoner. In the case of convicted criminals, three or four police officers would use several pieces of hemp rope at least ¼ inch (6 mm) in diameter and up to 80 feet (25 m) long.

If you want to restrain a burglar and you do not have 80 feet (24 m) of rope, take a piece of string, or even a shoelace, and tie his thumbs together behind his back. You could use a handcuff knot (see page 92) finished off with a square knot (see page 74), but make sure to pull all of the loops good and tight.

Hojojutsu relies on clever understanding of human anatomy. The ropes are positioned to restrict leverage, discourage struggle, and immobilize. There are specific rules:

The prisoner must not be able to escape.
The prisoner must not suffer any injury.
The prisoner must not see the technique.
The result must be aesthetically beautiful.

— Nawa Yumio, *Studies on Jitte and Torinawa* (1964).

Capturing an Opponent Traditional rope binding is done without the use of knots. However, the prisoner will still not be able to escape.

How to Tie a Hojojutsu String Ball

This is a useful way to wrap a long piece of string into a bundle from which you can pull it smoothly without either jamming or tangling.

1 Hold one end of the string between the finger and thumb of your left hand, with your palm facing you and the string hanging down.

2 Take the long end behind your little finger and then around underneath.

3 Bring the long end up the front, behind your first finger, and down the front again.

4 Repeat steps 2 and 3, making figure eights, until you are only about 9 inches (23 cm) from the end. Slide the loops carefully off your fingers, and hold them in your left hand while you wind the remaining string tightly around the middle. Tuck the last turn under the previous one, and pull tight to lock it in place.

5 Now when you want a length of string, pull the first end gently, and the string will come smoothly out of the bundle.

Loopy
Science

Physical string has helped in discoveries and inventions over the centuries, from parachutes to moving pictures. Today conceptual string and rope are at the forefront of science and discovery.

Discoveries and Inventions

By now you already have an inkling of string's measure in math and science. The ancient Egyptians pioneered the use of string for surveying (see page 20), using it to calculate accurate straight lines and right angles, while the Greek mathematicians Archimedes and Pythagoras used it to develop their famous theorems (see pages 26–27). Next you'll find out how visionaries such as Leonardo da Vinci, Galileo Galilei, and Benjamin Franklin employed string and rope in their many calculations and inventions.

String and Science

String and rope have powered the imagination of mathematicians and scientists around the world. In space, high-tech ropelike propulsion systems are being explored (see page 155) and the secrets of the Sun's giant magnetic ropes are revealed.

Simple Stringy Experiments

Not all string-based science requires a master's degree, a spacecraft, or an orbiting Hadron collider. Try this simple experiment in basic chemistry:

To grow crystals on a string, fill a cup with boiling water, and stir in your chosen chemical — epsom salts, alum, or sugar — until no more will dissolve; this mixture is called a saturated solution. Pour the solution into a jar with a string hanging into the water — a half-inch (1.3 cm) should be submerged. Different chemicals will produce their own uniquely shaped crystals.

Scientific Stringy Terminology

String can mean different things. The following are not actually string at all.

Computer Strings. To a computer programmer, a string is an ordered sequence of symbols storing data bytes. These strings organize — and help retrieve — the enormous amount of information stored on computers.

String Theory. A complex quantum physics theory (see page 154).

The Future of Rope and String

Cordage companies are exploring clever textile developments to create wonderful new products. These include the world's strongest rope and intelligent ropes that will track and monitor the stress on loads. In just one example, for an exhibition on extreme textiles at the Cooper-Hewitt Museum in New York, leading high performance ropemakers Yale Cordage and the innovative engineering firm SQUID Labs collaborated to produce a rope that was braided from electronic fibers to form the strings of an interactive musical rope harp.

Parachute Cord Modern parachute cord is made from nylon and has a tensile strength of 550 pounds (250 kg). Known as 550 paracord, it consists of 14 inner strings and a braided outer core, and is available in a range of colors: white, black, olive drab, and red. As well as being used for parachutes, this versatile cord is an essential part of any survival kit. It has myriad uses from rigging up a shelter to lashing together twigs to make snowshoes.

In the early morning hours around the campfire, enthusiasts also braid paracord to make decorative or functional items, such as bracelets and lanyards that can be quickly and easily unbraided in case they need to use the cord in an emergency situation.

Parachutes

Although the invention of the parachute was claimed by Jean-Pierre Blanchard, the French aviator in the eighteenth century, an early parachute design was in existence in the fifteenth century. Its creator was none other than the world-famous Italian genius and all-around Renaissance man Leonardo da Vinci. Although he is most well-known for his famous painting, *Mona Lisa*, da Vinci was a prolific inventor who was centuries ahead of time. In addition to designs for a parachute and prototype helicopter, he drew sketches for a ropemaking machine, rope-operated pulleys, and a crossbow.

The First Parachute Da Vinci devised a parachute design in which he claimed anyone could jump from any height without injury — since airplanes did not exist at the time, this would have meant leaping out of trees, or from cliffs or tall buildings. The chute itself was made from a linen fabric and was held in place by long wooden poles — in a similar manner to an umbrella frame.

In 1617, Croatian Faust Vrancic constructed a rigid-framed device based on da Vinci's drawing and jumped from a Venice tower wearing it. In 1785, Leonardo's design was improved on by French "aeronaut" Jean-Pierre Blanchard, who developed a foldable silk parachute for balloonists. By the late nineteenth century the harness and the concept of packing the parachute into a container were introduced. However, it was not until 1920 that the modern fold-up parachute with a ripcord was patented.

In 2000, the British skydiver Adrian Nichols tested Leonardo's design, jumping from a hot-air balloon at 10,000 feet (3,000 m). Nichols claimed that the experience was smoother than the modern parachute. However, at 2,000 feet (600 m) he cut away Leonardo's parachute and deployed a second modern parachute to avoid injury from the heavy, ancient device.

Flying High The parachute imagined by Leonardo da Vinci had a rigid frame that resembled an umbrella.

Seismographs

China has always been prone to earthquakes, so it makes sense that it was the Chinese who built the first earthquake detectors, or seismometers. The most celebrated version was built in 132 CE by scientist Chang Heng. It consisted of a cylindrical bronze jar about 7 feet (2 m) high, and it was decorated around the outside with eight dragons, who each stood above eight toads waiting directly underneath. Each dragon held a bronze ball in its mouth. If a ball fell off a dragon's mouth into the mouth of one of the eight toads below, it meant there had been an earthquake in the direction the dragon was facing.

How Does a Seismograph Work? All seismographs work through inertia. For example, in the seismograph on page 145, when you push the table, the whole thing will move for a fraction of a second. But the heavy bottle will stay where it is, because of inertia. However, the movement of the table gave a sideways tweak, so after a short pause the bottle will move, too, and it will swing to and fro.

The Chinese seismograph had an inverted pendulum inside, and when an earthquake shook the jar, the pendulum stayed still. So in effect, it moved toward the source of the shock, knocking the bronze ball out of the dragon's mouth.

Modern Seismographs The first modern seismograph was a horizontal pendulum seismograph invented by English scientist John Milne in 1880. After World War II this was improved and updated in the form of the Press-Ewing seismograph, which was developed in the United States for recording long-period waves. It records waves at least 500 miles (800 km) in length, and is still popular throughout the world today.

How to Make a Seismograph

You can build a simple version of the device without any bronze, dragons, or even toads. You will need a plastic bottle with a screw cap, such as one that contained water or cola, sticky tape, a little cardboard from a cereal box, a pen (ballpoint or marker), paper, and, of course, string.

1 Cut out a corner of the cardboard box so that you have a 6-inch (15 cm) horizontal strip, a 4-inch (10 cm) vertical strip, and a triangle connecting the two and holding them rigid.

2 Carefully tape the horizontal strip to the bottle and under the base of the bottle so that the vertical strip is 3 inches (7.5 cm) away. Tape the pen to the vertical strip.

3 Make a small hole in the bottle cap (with a hammer and nail, or a skewer). Feed the end of your piece of string down through the hole, and tie a good stopper knot (for example, a double overhand, see page 71) in the end.

4 Fill the bottle to the neck with water, screw on the cap, and suspend the bottle on the edge of a table, or the back of a chair, so that the bottle is just above the floor and the pen rests on the floor. Put a piece of paper under the pen.

5 Now you are ready to detect an earthquake. If you hit the table or chair from above, nothing much will happen. Quake waves move through the ground horizontally, rather than vertically. So if you give the table or chair a sideways shove or kick, you will get a big wiggle on the paper. The bigger the wiggle, the bigger the quake. Even better, if you can persuade a friend to move the paper slowly sideways while you make the quake, you will get the pattern real seismographs produce — a diminishing sine wave.

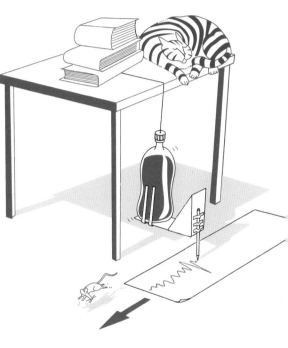

Measuring an Earthquake with String If you vibrate a weighted string suspended from a table, it will produce an earthquake-like wave on a homemade seismograph.

Pendulums

In the 1580s, a young medical student named Galileo Galilei was sitting in a cathedral in Pisa, Italy. Bored by a long sermon, he watched a great bronze lamp hanging from the glorious ceiling on a long chain. As it swung back and forth in the draft, he measured the time of each swing against his pulse, since watches had not yet been invented. To his surprise, he found that the lamp always took the same time for each swing, whether it moved several feet from side to side or just an inch or two.

How Does a Pendulum Work? The period of the pendulum — the time it takes for a complete swing from left to right and right to left — does not depend on either the size of the swing (as long as it isn't too wide) or the heaviness of the weight, but rather only on the length of the string. To double the period of time it takes for a swing, you need a string four times as long.

We now know the period of a pendulum is determined by the formula $P = 2\pi\sqrt{l/g}$ where l is the length of the pendulum and g is the acceleration due to gravity. Therefore, Galileo was right.

How Did Galileo Use His Discovery? Galileo invented a neat little pendulum pulse meter he could use to check his patients, but the medical authorities stole his idea and exploited it.

Galileo also pointed out that the pendulum, being a reliable timekeeper, would be an excellent basis for a precise clock. He even designed a pendulum clock, but he was busy studying the science of falling and gazing at the heavens through his telescope, and he did not get around to making his clock before he died in 1642. The first pendulum clock was built by the Dutch scientist Christiaan Huygens in 1657.

Imaginary Pendulums

Galileo discovered the principle
of the pendulum while sitting
in a cathedral in Pisa, Italy. We
don't know if he tested it from
the leaning tower, but it is nice
to imagine that he did.

Lightning Conductors

String played a significant part in the invention of the lightning conductor by American founding father and all-around polymath Benjamin Franklin. Franklin wanted to prove his theory that lightning was an electrical phenomenon, not a punishment from God, as was believed by many at the time.

One stormy night in 1752, he attached a wire and a long hemp string to a silk kite and launched it into the thunderstorm. Franklin knew that if he held onto the string he would get a shock, so he tied a silk ribbon to the string and held the ribbon. And he fastened a metal key to the end of the string so that the electricity went into the key. The wire attracted the lightning, but silk doesn't conduct electricity, so the hemp string carried the electricity to the key. When Franklin put his knuckle near the key he got a shock, demonstrating that metal was a good conductor and inspiring Franklin to invent the lightning rod.

Don't try this at home, folks: Franklin was knocked unconscious twice when he was experimenting with electricity. German scientist Georg Wilhelm Richmann was far less fortunate with his stormy investigations; he was electrocuted and killed when a lightning ball struck him in 1753. He is believed to be the first person to have died while conducting electrical experiments.

Lightning Conductors Today Modern lightning conductors, or lightning rods, are metal strips that are usually made of copper or aluminum. They are often erected on rooftops, where they form just part of much bigger lightning protection systems. These systems often consist of connections from the rooftop to the ground and also bond connections to metallic objects within the conductors. Lightning protection systems are installed on buildings, trees, and bridges. In some parts of the world, the conductors are still sometimes referred to as "Franklin rods."

A Lightning Experiment
Franklin's famous experiment
with his kite led to the first
lightning conductor, or
lightning rod, for diverting
electricity into the ground.

Moving Pictures

The first moving pictures were produced by an eccentric Englishman who began life in Kingston-on-Thames, England, as Edward Muggeridge. However, at the age of 25 he moved to San Francisco, California, and changed his name to the grander-sounding Eadweard Muybridge. Muybridge's machinery used string and came about as a result of a puzzled politician's commission.

Solving a Mystery In 1872, Leland Stanford, the governor of California, hired Muybridge to settle a bet: Did a galloping horse ever have all four hoofs off the ground at the same time? To the naked eye the action was much too fast to be sure. After several experiments, Muybridge set up a row of 24 cameras that were 10 inches (24 cm) apart along a racetrack. Each camera's shutter was fired by a trip string he had stretched across the track. As the horse galloped past, it kicked through the strings and took 24 successive pictures of its own hoofs during a single stride. When played back in succession on an ingenious projector system called a zoopraxiscope, the pictures showed that all four hoofs were off the ground at one point in each stride.

The Galloping Question
Muybridge found the answer to the question "Does a galloping horse ever have all four hoofs off the ground?" with his invention of the zoopraxiscope — the forerunner of the movie projector.

Muybridge went on to photograph other animals moving, as well as men and women in various states of undress. There is a sequence of a woman walking along, artfully dropping a scarf and picking it up again, and dramatic sequences of naked men running and playing sports. Muybridge became rich and famous, and his success all began with 24 pieces of string.

Stringy Theories

String and rope have been involved in a wide range of scientific theories. Some of these ideas have proved to be spectacular failures, while others have been world-changing successes. Next you'll discover examples of both cases.

Steering a Balloon

An early champion of the theory of steering balloons was S. A. Andrée — a Swedish civil engineer, explorer, and balloonist — some might say a balloonatic, because he experimented with steering hydrogen-filled balloons by means of drag ropes. He used this technique when he set off with two others toward the North Pole in 1897.

The Expedition Andrée's plan was to dangle heavy, long ropes from the balloon. These would both prevent the balloon from flying too high and slow its progress, so that instead of merely drifting in the same direction as the wind, he hoped to steer by using sails — just as a sailboat can be steered because it is held back by pushing through the water.

Andrée assumed that he could rely on the wind blowing more-or-less in the right direction (north), so that he could fine-tune his course with his drag ropes and sails. No modern balloonist has expressed any faith in such a system. Andrée's claims were based on wishful thinking, on the effects of variable winds, and on the fact that most of the time he was in the clouds and had no idea which way he was going. There were technical problems, too. His drag ropes frequently fell off, or broke. Sometimes the two would get tangled together. And sometimes one or both would snag immovably on a post, tree, or iceberg, which brought the balloon down in a terrifying and dangerous bounce. Andrée's balloon crashed on the pack ice after only two days.

Rope Steerage Andrée's experiment to show that a balloon could be steered by ropes failed, and the balloon crashed in the Arctic. All three balloonists survived the crash but died during their walk home. Their remains, notes, and photographs were found approximately 35 years later.

String Theory

Developed and refined by many distinguished academics during the twentieth century, string theory is where math meets quantum physics. Why is this complex branch of quantum physics named after string? At its base, it is because the theory holds that the particles that make up the universe are constantly oscillating under tension, rather like the strings of a guitar. And if you could see an electron or a quark — the building blocks of the universe — under a microscope, it would resemble a tiny loop of oscillating string. So the world is made of string, vibrating in 11 dimensions. How does string theory work? If you want to find out more about the theory, visit its official website: www.superstringtheory.com

Solar Energy Ropes On May 20, 2007, NASA's THEMIS mission spacecraft fleet detected giant magnetic ropes that connect Earth's upper atmosphere to the Sun. These ropes are formed from bundles of magnetic fields that are twisted like a mariner's rope. Scientists believe that solar particles flow along these ropes, powering geomagnetic storms and auroras such as the northern lights. Mysteriously, some ancient cultures have tales of rope and strings tying the Earth to the Sun.

What does THEMIS mean? It stands for Time History of Events and Macroscale Interactions during Substorms. Try stringing that tongue twister together fast.

A Model Knitter

It may surprise you to know that theoretical mathematicians use yarn and the crafts of crochet and knitting to model geometric shapes. Alan Turing, the father of modern computer science, is said to have knitted Möbius strips and other geometric shapes during his lunch break.

Tether Propulsion System

One of the most ambitious uses planned for rope is to haul people and other payloads into space, thus avoiding the use of expensive rockets, by a system called HASTOL (Hypersonic Airplane Space Tether Orbital Launch).

How Does HASTOL Work? Imagine a cowboy galloping along, whirling his lariat. The lasso is moving faster than him on one side, where he is whirling it forward. But on the other side it is going more slowly and, with luck, at just the right speed to drop over the head of a trotting steer. In the same way, a small space station in low Earth orbit, perhaps 940 miles (1,500 km) above ground, will have a rope 875 miles (1,400 km) long whirling around forward out into space and then backward down toward the Earth. At that altitude the orbital speed has to be about 15,500 miles (25,000 km) per hour. But at its nearest point to the Earth, the tip of the spinning rope is moving backward at about 6,300 miles (10,000 km) per hour relative to the spacecraft, which means that its speed relative to the ground is only about 9,000 miles (14,500 km) per hour, or Mach 12. This is slow enough to match the speed of an aircraft — a Boeing DF-9 aircraft can deliver a payload of 14 tons to an altitude of 60 miles (96.5 km) at Mach 12.

What Type of Rope? The rope would be a special open, tubular net made up of perhaps 20 primary lines, with diagonal ties of thinner lines designed to take the strain if a primary line were blown away by an asteroid collision. The lines would be made of polymeric material, thick near the center, but tapering toward the end to save weight. And they would have heat-resistant tips that would not burn in the thin atmosphere, and an aluminum wire inside to generate power as the lines sweep through Earth's magnetic field, providing information and control for the earthbound operators.

Space Elevator

If you think the HASTOL space launch system (see page 155) is an impossible dream, then you will probably think the space elevator is out of this world. In reality, it is actually a simpler idea, although it seems even more outrageous.

How Does a Space Elevator Work?
An asteroid is tethered to an incredibly tall tower by an extra-long rope or cable that carries an elevator. The idea is that the center of mass of the asteroid and the cable should be 22,000 miles (33,405 km) above the Earth in a "geostationary" orbit. Spacecraft in low Earth orbit — say 200 miles (321 km) up — go around the world in about 90 minutes. The farther out the orbit, the longer the orbiting time, until at 22,000 miles (33,405 km) the spacecraft takes just 24 hours to go around the Earth. This is called a geostationary orbit, because any object orbiting at that distance above the equator appears to be hovering without moving.

Television and other communications satellites are placed in geostationary orbits, which is why if you have a satellite dish, it points toward the equator — south in the northern hemisphere and north in the southern hemisphere, and it does not have to move or change its aiming point.

Now the cable, along with its asteroid anchor, is in orbit around the Earth, and it goes straight up from the 30-mile high (48 km) tower constructed at the equator. The final step is to mount elevators on the cable and power them by electromagnetic induction, then tourists could be zoomed into space by the busload, without the need for expensive and dangerous rockets. The idea sounds incredible, but when Sir Arthur C. Clarke, who invented the geostationary satellite, was asked when it might become reality, he said, "Probably about 50 years after everybody quits laughing."

How to Make a Space Elevator

1 Build a tower somewhere on the equator that is about 30 miles (48 km) high.

2 Capture a multimillion-ton asteroid, and put it in orbit around the Earth.

3 Tether the asteroid to the top of the tower with a rope or cable that is about 22,000 miles (33,405 km) long.

Country
Ties

String and rope have many uses in the great outdoors, both on land and at sea. Without string, nets would not exist and fish would not be harvested. Without rope, seafaring would not have been possible, animals could not be tethered, and heavy loads could not be tied together and transported.

On Land

The use of string and rope on land is as old as agriculture itself — about 10,000 years, give or take a week or two.

Farming

From the earliest times, as soon as sheep, cows, yaks, and buffalo were domesticated, farmers all over the world used rope to tether them and contain them in pens and fields. They tied their produce in bundles with string; they used it to support their grapes, hops, and raspberries, and they even took rope to mark out the boundaries of their land.

Baling Twine All sorts of string and rope are used on farms. But one of the most characteristic and commonly used is baling twine, which is made of strands of polypropylene and is extraordinarily strong and useful stuff. It has been used for holding up pants (as a belt or suspenders), lacing shoes, repairing luggage, tethering dogs, holding barn doors together, and securing loads on bicycles and truck beds.

However, the primary job of baling twine is to secure bales of hay and straw. Both hay and straw are made from dried grasses. After the grasses have been harvested, they are dried, and then compressed into bales. The bales are tied together securely with two lengths of baling twine.

These bales are not only rugged enough to be stacked in barns for the winter, providing a plentiful store of fodder to feed animals, but are also strong enough to build houses, supplying excellent insulation.

Making Hay String had more technical uses as well, as we see in this lively instruction for making hay from *Fitzherbert's Book of Husbandry*, first published about 1523 in England. No one knows whether the author was Sir Anthony Fitzherbert or his elder brother John:

When thy meadow be mowed, they would be well tedded [spread out] and laid even upon the ground. Turn it clean before noon, as soon as the dew is gone. And if thou dare trust the weather, let it lie so all night: and on the next day, turn it again before noon. And for to know when it has withered enough, make a little rope of the same, that ye think should be the most greenest, and twine it as hard together between your hands as ye can, and so being twon, let one take a knife and cut it fast by your hand; and the knots will be moist if it be not dry enough.

So now you know how to make hay. I particularly like the word twon, which means "twined."

Tree Ropes Climbing trees can be a paid job — arborists (sometimes known as tree surgeons) trim or cut down overgrown trees, on farmland, in parks, in domestic yards, and on managed forestry plots. Custom ropes are made for them. These are usually fabricated from lightweight, braided polyester, and they are designed to be nonsnagging, and resistant to abrasion, rot, and mildew. Rope also is used to make rope ladders for access to tree houses, and is used in tree adventure courses.

Towropes You may not find one of these in the trunk of an automobile these days, but farmers always keep a towrope handy to move machinery around their land with a tractor. Today's high-tech synthetic towropes are resistant to chemicals, such as diesel fuel and fertilizer, making them more durable than nylon rope. They are less stretchy, too, so they are safer because they are less likely to recoil when a vehicle suddenly stops.

Plowing with Rope Before planting begins for the next season, the ground needs to be prepared. The first farmers probably used pointed sticks to scratch the earth, but then they discovered they could use animals to pull an early form of plow called an ard across the fields, saving themselves a lot of "ard" work. The simplest ard was a forked tree branch cut to the proper shape and pulled by an ox or a donkey. Later came plows with wheels, but the critical thing was that they all needed to be pulled with a rope.

Thousands of years later, in 1854 to be precise, the Royal Agricultural Society of England offered a prize of £500 (around $141,276 in today's money) for the best steam-powered plowing machine, and in 1858 John Fowler won the prize. Fowler's machine consisted of a huge steam engine planted at one side of the field and an anchor carriage on the opposite side. The plow was moved back and forth on a long rope pulled by a windlass on the engine; the rope was later replaced by a steel cable. Getting the heavy engine to the right place across soft fields was difficult,

Ard Work The earliest plow was made from a tree branch and a length of rope.

but the plowing was fast and efficient. When internal combustion engines arrived, tractors took over many tasks on the farm and ropes were no longer needed.

Animal Husbandry

Rope and string are used in many different ways by those who work with animals.

Birthing Rope On a farm it seems that there are always cows calving or sheep lambing. Sometimes animals need a helping hand from the farmer or a veterinarian during the delivery of their young, and a vital piece of equipment in that process is the birthing rope. The farmer or vet ties a bowline knot (see page 94) in a nylon rope, pushes his hand into the mother, and slips the bowline around the forelegs of the baby animal inside her. Then he steps back and gives the baby a good tug to help it out into the cold world.

Rope Lead The simplest way to lead an animal is by means of a rope with a loop around its neck. This needs to be a thick rope — at least ½ an inch (1.2 cm) if possible — and tied in a bowline (see page 94), which will not slip. Never use a slip knot, which can tighten and choke the animal. Most horse tack is made of leather, but normal rope is sometimes used for the reins, and most often for halters or lead ropes.

The unpleasant Geier hitch is used to control powerful animals such as bulls. A rope is tied to the nose ring, and then tightened along the stomach, and around the scrotum and testicles. If the animal starts running, bucking, or throwing its head, the constriction and pain caused by the rope soon persuades it to stop. A round turn and two half hitches (see page 86) is used to avoid the danger of serious injury.

Barbed Wire Devil's rope was what its early opponents called barbed wire. It was the invention that really tamed the American West — the six-gun was a poor second. Cattlemen had to contain their herds; wooden fencing was too expensive, and in some places timber was scarce. Ordinary wire was of no use; cows could break through just by leaning on it. Something fiercer was required. Farmers tried various ideas, but it was not until 1874 when Joseph F. Glidden of DeKalb, Illinois, produced a viable product.

Immediately dozens of others tried to jump on the bandwagon, and applications for 570 patents were filed for, leading eventually to more than 2,000 different types of barbed wire. However, Glidden's design was considered superior and he soon became known as the Father of Barbed Wire.

In 1876, salesman John Warne Gates traveled down from Illinois to San Antonio, Texas, to demonstrate the effectiveness of barbed wire. According to legend, he stood with a group of steers in a small barbed-wire enclosure and fired his gun. The cattle all charged outward and bounced off the fence. In the Menger Hotel bar that evening, Gates sold 80 miles (130 km) of barbed wire.

Electric String When farmers want to contain cows or sheep for a short time, but do not want to put up an expensive permanent barrier, they will usually use an electric fence. This consists of one or more strings (or tapes) suspended on insulated posts around a field.

The strings are made of stranded polyethylene or another synthetic material, with fine wire strands woven in between the polyethylene. The strings are connected at one end to a battery-powered electrical energizer unit, which delivers a high-voltage pulse along the wire about once a second. The pulses are extremely brief — less than a thousandth of a second — so they cannot do any permanent damage. If you take hold of the wire, you will feel an unpleasant jolt because you are grounding the fence; the current can pass through your body to the ground. When a cow or a sheep comes into contact with it — especially if the contact is with a wet nose — they, too, get a short, sharp shock. They quickly learn not to approach the fence again. So the electric fence works effectively as both a physical and a psychological barrier.

Ropy Dogs Down-to-earth farm dogs are often tethered or led with a simple piece of rope or string — fancy jeweled collars and fine leather leashes are for city dandies. A homemade country-style dog leash will serve you well in an emergency.

To make one, take a nylon rope, and melt both ends with a match. Fold over the end to make a loop, and tie an overhand knot (see page 70). Do the same with the other end, put one loop around the dog's neck, making sure it can't choke the animal, and the other around your wrist, and go.

Making a Rope Dog Toy

Dogs large and small, whether farm dogs or domestic pets, love playing tug-of-war. To make a suitable toy, take a length of cotton rope (avoid the synthetic type because this could damage your dog's gums), tie a knot at one end for you to hold and a simple noose (make sure that it can't slip) at the other for the dog to grab in its jaws. Holding the knot, throw the loop for the dog to fetch. Once he has it in his teeth, tug on the rope, and have fun wrestling against your dog for control of the rope.

How to Weigh a Pig Well, you can't actually weigh a pig, but according to *The Old Farmer's Almanac* (first published in 1792), you can estimate its weight accurately using only string. Here is what you do:

1 Use a string to measure the heart girth of the pig — the circumference just behind its front legs. Mark the string's circumference with an ink mark or an overhand knot (see page 70).

2 Measure the pig's length from the base of its ears to the base of its tail and mark that.

3 Convert both measurements to inches, using a tape measure. If you have don't have either at hand, use your own frame. Most people's wingspan (fingertip to fingertip) is equal to their height; so both my height and wingspan are 72 inches, and my half-span (fingertip to breastbone) is 36 inches. With thumb and forefinger I span 6 inches, with thumb and pinkie I span 9 inches. So if the length of the pig is half my wingspan less my thumb and forefinger handspan that is 30 inches.

4 Multiply the heart girth by itself and then the result by the length.

5 Divide by 400 if your pig is alive, or by 500 if it is dead, for the approximate weight of the pig in pounds. (For kilograms divide your result by 2.2.)

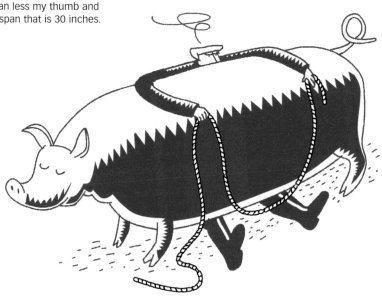

Cowboys The rope that is most often associated with cowboys is commonly known as a lasso, but the whole rope is really called a lariat. It is generally nylon, $\frac{5}{16}$ or $\frac{3}{8}$ of an inch (8 or 10 mm) in diameter, and stiff enough to retain its loop when the lasso is thrown. For trick roping, some swear by maguey, which is a four-strand rope, handmade from agave fibers, and very stiff. The noose itself uses a honda knot (see page 93). For tying down wild cattle and calves in the rodeo, cowboys use pigging string or hogging rope. To hold on their hats, they use stampede string. And reata or skin-string is a braided or twisted rawhide rope used for lariats.

Camping

In the past, tents of all kinds used guy ropes to secure them in the ground. Some of today's dome tents do not need guy ropes, but other modern tents have "glow in the dark" ropes so you don't trip over them in the night. Lashings are used to hold together two or more pieces of wood, which can be done in various ways (see below).

How to Make a Sheer Lashing To fix two pieces of wood together in order to make a longer piece — such as for a flagpole — you need to overlap them and lash them together.

1 Line up the timber pieces, side by side, overlapping them by at least six times their thickness. Secure your string with a clove hitch (see page 82), then wrap it around both pieces of wood. Make 8–10 turns around the two pieces of wood, keeping the string tight at all times. Secure a second length of string at the other end of the overlap; this second lashing stops movement in any direction.

2 Repeat the 8 to 10 turns with the second lashing. Secure both lashings by tying a clove hitch.

How to Make a Square Lashing To fix two pieces of wood together at right angles, use a square lashing:

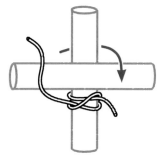

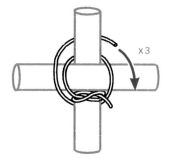

1 Tie the middle of the string to one piece of wood with a clove hitch (see page 82). Then lay the second piece of wood on top of the first.

2 Take both ends of the string over the second piece of wood and under the first piece, crossing over. Repeat three times.

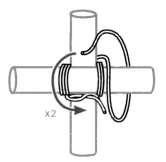

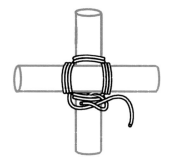

3 Take the string back over the first piece of wood. Repeat two times.

4 Finish with a square knot (see page 74), making sure that you keep the string tight.

How to Make a Jar Sling When you go hiking, camping, or fishing you probably carry a bottle of water with you. You can put the bottle in your backpack, but this uses valuable space — and you may not always want to take a backpack with you. Instead, try making a jar sling, which is best tied with a piece of thick string, thin cord, or rope. Start with a piece about 3 feet (1 m) long. This will work with any jar or bottle that has a bit of a neck, as long as you pull the sling tight. The sling technique looks tricky at first sight, but getting it right is not hard, and it is well worth it in the end.

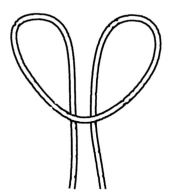

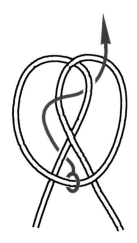

1 In the middle of the string make a pair of mirror-image loops, as shown. Cross one slightly over the other.

2 Put your thumb and finger down through the outside of the top loop, under the bottom loop, back over the top loop, then under the bottom loop. Grab the middle of the original loop and pull it all the way back through.

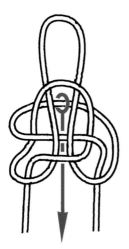

3 Pull the middle of what was the top loop down toward the long ends of the rope.

4 Pull the middle of what was the bottom loop down toward the long ends of the length of rope.

5 Carefully pull the top loop and the long ends, and the ring in the middle will tighten. Slip it over the top of your bottle, pull it tight, and you can use it to carry the bottle.

6 To make a carrying handle, tie the long loop to the long ends using an overhand bend knot (see page 80).

At Sea

Rope has been used by sailors for centuries: In a man-made cave at the ancient Red Sea port of Marsa Gawasis, archeologists found 60 tidy coils of strong vegetable fiber rope that had apparently been left there by sailors 4,000 years ago. One theory is that they were used to tie together the bow and stern of ships, although why they were stored in the cave remains a mystery.

Marine Rope and Cord

Ropes hold up ship's sails, and secure boats at a mooring or by reeling down to the sea floor with an anchor. And string is knotted into nets to catch fish and hammocks for sailors to catch some zzzz.

Hammocks String-net beds, which were suspended at each end, are where sailors used to sleep on the ship. These utilitarian beds known as hammocks would be slung between the bulkheads, and three sailors, one above another, would often have to share a cramped space barely 4 feet (1.2 m) high. However, under less stressful conditions hammocks are relaxing and fun. They are light, comfortable, and take up little space. The word hammock is believed to have come from the South American word *hamack* — the name of the tree whose bark the Maya people used to weave their beds.

Real hammocks are like nets, made from approximately 4,000 feet (1,200 m) of string — usually hemp or jute, since these materials hold knots well, and are relatively soft to lie on. Making a hammock is a complex process and takes some time.

You can make your own more simply. Find some convenient trees in your yard, about 10 or 12 feet (3 m or 3.6 m) apart. Take 30 feet (9 m) of rope, tie the middle to one tree with a clove hitch (see page 82), and tie both ends to the next tree using round turns and two half hitches (see page 86). Then push two wooden spreaders between the ropes. These are battens about 18 inches

(45 cm) long with a V-cut into each end, so that they hold the ropes apart, one at the head end and one at the feet. Next find an old blanket and lay one end across both ropes, take the rest of the blanket underneath both ropes, and then back across both ropes, to make a place to lie. Finally, carefully climb in (this can sometimes be tricky) and fall asleep.

Salty Rope Terminology Every rope on a boat has a specific name to help sailors avoid mistakes.

The **foot rope** is what sailors stand on while furling sails.

The **tiller rope** controls the tiller and holds the boat on course.

A **downhaul** pulls downward on a sail to increase the tension.

A **yard** is a wooden spar that is hung horizontally across a mast and from which a sail hangs.

Braces are lines, or ropes, attached to the yard for turning or trimming the sail. The **mainbrace** was the largest, heaviest, and most important brace.

To "splice the mainbrace" was to issue an extra shot of rum. If the mainbrace was shot away by the enemy it had to be mended — the ship was unsteerable without it. Splicing the mainbrace to repair it was one of the most difficult jobs onboard, which was why it became traditional to award the seamen who did it an extra drink.

Ship's Rigging

Rigging is the apparatus a ship needs to use the power of the wind to move forward. There are two types: standing rigging, to hold up the masts, and running rigging, to control the sails. A good example of a rigged sailing ship was legendary British Admiral Horatio Nelson's flagship, HMS *Victory*, launched in 1765. It had 27 miles (43 km) of rigging and a total of 37 sails, covering an area of 1.3 acres (half a hectare). Its mainbrace was 5 inches (13 cm) thick.

Running Rigging Sailors use running rigging on a ship to raise, lower, and control the sails. Running rigging must be flexible in order to allow for the smooth movement of the spars and sails, but it needs to be strong enough for the role it plays. In the past even a landlubber could tell the difference between standing rigging and running rigging. The standing rigging, which held up the masts, was coated with tar for preservation, so it was dark brown. The running rigging was untarred and much lighter in color, because tarred rope was too stiff to handle. Today, with luck, you can still tell the difference, because the standing rigging is often made of steel cable, while the running rigging is usually made of polyester rope.

The running rigging of traditional sailing ships, like the one shown right, was a complex system, containing separate wonderfully named elements, which are listed below. In a small sailing boat today, you need a halyard to hoist anything up a mast. And to pull the corner of a sail, you need a sheet. Note that a "sheet" is a rope, not a sail; the mainsail is controlled by the mainsheet.

KEY

1. Flying jib guys
2. Standing jib guys
3. Spritsail lifts
4. Spritsail braces
5. Main yard tackles
6. Fore lifts
7. Fore braces
8. Main lifts
9. Main braces
10. Cross-jack lifts
11. Cross-jack braces
12. Fore topsail lifts
13. Fore topsail braces
14. Main topsail lifts
15. Main topsail braces
16. Mizzen topsail lifts
17. Mizzen topsail braces
18. Main topgallant lifts
19. Main topgallant braces
20. Main topgallant halyards
21. Fore topsail halyards
22. Main topsail halyards
23. Mizzen topsail halyards
24. Foremast halyards
25. Mainmast halyards
26. Mizzen yard brace
27. Mizzen vangs

Standing Rigging The standing rigging is what holds up the masts on a ship. Some ships had as many as six masts, each of them made from one or two tree trunks. The only way to hold them upright was to tie them to the hull of the ship with ropes in all directions, just like the guy ropes on a tent. The same technique is used today for radio masts and flagpoles. On modern boats the standing rigging is usually made of steel cable. The ropes or steel wires used for standing rigging are not moved or changed; they stay in place, which is why it is called "standing." The most important elements of standing rigging in a traditional sailing ship shown at right are given below.

KEY

1. Bobstays
2. Bowsprit shrouds
3. Fore shrouds
4. Main shrouds
5. Mizzen shrouds
6. Fore preventer stay and Forestay
7. Main preventer stay and Mainstay
8. Mizzen stay
9. Fore topmast rigging
10. Main topmast rigging
11. Mizzen topmast rigging
12. Fore topmast standing backstays
13. Main topmast standing backstays
14. Mizzen topmast backstay
15. Fore topmast preventer stay and fore-top-mast stay
16. Main topmast preventer stay
17. Main topmast stay
18. Mizzen topmast stay
19. Fore topgallant rigging
20. Main topgallant rigging
21. Mizzen topgallant rigging
22. Fore topgallant standing backstay
23. Main topgallant standing backstay
24. Mizzen topgallant backstay
25. Fore topgallant stay
26. Main topgallant stay
27. Mizzen topgallant stay
28. Fore royal backstay
29. Main royal backstay
30. Mizzen royal backstay
31. Fore royal stay
32. Main royal stay
33. Mizzen royal stay
34. Standing jib stay
35. Flying jib stay
36. Martingale
37. Fore futtock shrouds
38. Main futtock shrouds
39. Mizzen futtock shrouds

Fishing Nets

Fishing nets are simply loads of string tying together holes that are too small for the fish to swim through. They range from little shrimping nets designed for children, to vast enclosures thousands of feet or meters long drifting through the sea. Traditionally, nets were made from hemp or other natural fibers soaked in tar to help preserve them. Today, most nets are made from synthetic materials such as nylon, which are stronger and rot proof.

The Drift Net This net may be many miles or kilometers long and 200 feet (60 m) deep. The top edge is supported by floats, and the bottom edge is weighted down. The net is dragged slowly through the water by a pair of ships called drifters, and it will catch almost anything swimming close to the surface. Because they often net porpoises, turtles, and other things that are not fish, drift nets are banned in many parts of the world.

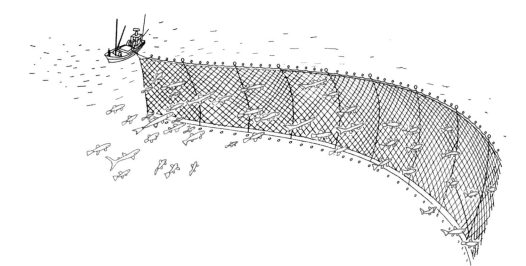

The Purse Seine Net This net is similar to the drift type, but much smaller. A single ship pulls it into a complete circle, so that it surrounds a shoal of fish swimming near the surface—such as anchovies, sardines, herring, and mackerel. When the circle is complete, the bottom edge of the net is pulled together with a rope (like a purse with a drawstring) to prevent the fish from escaping underneath, and the whole net is pulled onboard the ship.

The Trawl Net Dragged behind a stern trawler or a pair of trawlers, the trawl net may be arranged to catch shoals of shrimp, tuna, and mackerel swimming at moderate depths, or cod, halibut, and squid who are near the sea bottom. The fish collect in the back of the net as the ship moves forward; then the entire net is hoisted onboard.

Loose
Ends

String Miscellany

Here are a couple of extra strands of knowledge to tie to your new, extensive knowledge of string and rope. You'll find string-related items that have made the news. And, for string fanatics, there are some useful websites, too.

String in the News

One way or another, string and rope always seem to wind their way through our culture. Here are some curiosities you might not know.

Stringers Freelance news operators are known as "stringers." They hunt out a raft of local stories with wide appeal and spread them around the world by selling them to different networks.

String Cheats String cheats go to vending machines and feed in a dollar bill attached to a piece of fishing line or tape. When they have the merchandise, they carefully pull the money back out of the machine. One company has installed a lamp that generates a beam of polarized light. This detector is able to spot the line or tape, and it activates both a guillotine to cut it and an alarm to alert security staff.

Burning Rope Stunt British escapologist Shahid Malik was strapped into a straitjacket and suspended from a crane on a burning rope 160 feet (48 m) above the center of Glasgow, Scotland. He wriggled his way free in three minutes.

The End of the String Tank? The string tank was designed by a Norwegian Army officer who joined fishing nets together. As long as there is a layer on top, the gaps between the strings trap air, which is a good insulator, and keeps the wearer warm. The string tank has been championed by Madonna, and a number of American rappers, but may be going out of fashion.

Rap Up in a String Tank

Insulation with air is the thing
To make winter feel warm as the spring
So invest in a layer
Of lovely warm air
Trapped in holes, tied together with string.

Stringy Websites

Here are some websites for additional information on some stringy and ropy subjects.

www.ayya.org
The American Yo-Yo Association (AYYA) is a membership organization that promotes yo-yo activity in the United States.

www.bindertwine.ca
Kleinburg Village in Ontario, Canada, holds an annual binder twine festival, complete with a binder twine queen contest.

www.christojeanneclaude.net
Official site of the artist who wraps architecture and landscape in fabric and string.

www.darwintwineball.com
Official site of the Darwin Twine Ball Museum in Darwin, Minnesota, devoted to the largest twine ball made by one man.

www.fontspace.com/category/twine
Free twine fonts for the string obsessed.

www.girlscouts.org
Official website of the Girl Scouts of America, offering a wide range of programs for girls and young women aged 5 to 25.

www.hempmuseum.org
The site of the U.S.A. Hemp Museum is dedicated to all things hemp. It has a virtual room entirely devoted to rope and twine, as well as photographs of examples from around the world.

www.hms-victory.com

Official website for Admiral Horatio Nelson's flagship, HMS *Victory*, which is best known for her role in the Battle of Trafalgar. Find out about the men who sailed in her, how she was built, and her long and continuing Naval career.

www.igkt.net

The International Guild of Knot Tyers (IGKT) is a nonprofit organization of people with interests in knots and knotting techniques of all kinds. Membership is open to anyone who is interested in knotting.

www.isfa.org

The International String Figure Association (ISFA) is a small, nonprofit organization whose primary goal is to gather, preserve, and distribute string-figure knowledge. The only requirement for joining is enthusiasm and a passion for making string figures!

www.lusterleaf.com/GardenTwine/GardenTwine.htm

A leading U.S. supplier of garden products, including all-purpose garden twine made from both natural and synthetic fibers.

www.nasa.gov/mission_pages/themis/main/

Official government NASA website, which contains detailed information about THEMIS (Time History of Events and Macroscale Interactions), a mission investigating solar ropes and changes in auroras in the Earth's atmosphere (see page 154).

www.neropes.com

New England Ropes, manufacturer of high-quality baler twine, polypropylene strapping, and a wide range of industrial, climbing, and marine ropes.

www.pan-ams.org

The Pan American Rope Skipping Organization (PARSO) promotes rope skipping in the Americas, and provides athletes with opportunities to develop and experience cross-cultural training and competition.

www.plymouthcordagemuseum.org

A museum run by the Plymouth Cordage Historical Society. You can tour the historic nineteenth-century ropemaking mill of the Plymouth Cordage Co., and visit the workers' housing.

www.ropecord.com

Official website of the Cordage Institute — an association of rope, twine and related manufacturers, their suppliers, and affiliated industries. Its aim is to provide safety standards and to educate government agencies and product users on the correct and proper use of rope in industry.

www.rosaryline.ca

Make your own prayer rope (see page 32), or you can shop for a handmade rosary.

www.scouting.org

Official website of the Boy Scouts of America, offering year-round programs for boys aged 7 to 17 and mixed programs for young people up to the age of 25.

www.scouts.ca/dnn

Official website of Scouts Canada — the country's leading youth organization, offering programs for boys, girls, and young people aged 5 to 26.

www.shoe-lacing.com

A fun website that looks at the fashion and science of shoelacing. It includes instructions on 36 ways to tie shoes and boots.

www.skyways.lib.ks.us/towns/Cawker/twine.html

The Cawker City ball (see page 60) is the world's largest sisal twine ball to be made by a group effort; string is added every year at the Twine-a-thon festival. To visit the festival see www.travelks.com.

www.stringartfun.com

Imaginative and fun ideas for creating pictures with nails and string. There are useful tips on string art techniques, as well as patterns to download, and string art pictures you can buy.

www.stringfigure.com

Imaginative string figures from Hawaii, including patterns, stories and mythology connected with this ancient art. There also is an online store where you can buy healing necklaces, lei, and DVDs.

www.superstringtheory.com

Official website explaining all you need to know about the complex quantum physics string theory and how it works. If you're scientifically minded, this one's for you!

www.theiff.org/reef

Official website of the Institute For Figuring (the IFF) — an educational organization dedicated to enhancing the understanding of figures and figuring techniques.

www.yalecordage.com

Suppliers of rope for use in sailing, tree surgery, and industry.

Index

Author's Acknowledgments

First and foremost I would like to thank Judith More, mistress of the Fil Rouge Press, for asking me to write this book, and for encouraging me when I flagged. Many thanks too, to Chauncy Dunford for doing much of the initial research, to Hannah Boyd for taking over the research and driving the project while Judith was in Frankfurt, to Miren for her excellent work on the text, to 'OME Design for their splendid design, and especially to Paul Boston for his superb pictures and wicked sense of humor. Without them this book simply would not have happened.

The publisher would like to thank

Adam and Paul for unraveling this eccentric idea so neatly and entertainingly in their wonderful words and pictures.

Thanks, too, to editors and researchers Miren, Chauncy, and Hannah and designers Martin and Jilly for stringing together the pages so successfully, and to Kim, Jen, and George for reeling them into North American mode so cleverly.

Last but not least, many thanks to Dolores and Katie for believing in the potential of a little piece of string and helping us turn it into a book.